The Integrated Self-Advocacy ISA™ Curriculum

A Program for Emerging Self-Advocates with Autism Spectrum and Other Conditions

Teacher Edition

Valerie Paradiz, Ph.D.

Foreword by Stephen Shore, Ed.D.

APC

P.O. Box 23173
Shawnee Mission, Kansas 66283-0173
www.asperger.net

Autism Asperger Publishing Co.
P.O. Box 23173
Shawnee Mission, Kansas 66283-0173
www.asperger.net

Publisher's Cataloging-in-Publication

Paradiz, Valerie, 1963-
     The integrated self-advocacy curriculum : a program for emerging
     self-advocates with autism spectrum and other conditions / Valerie
     Paradiz ; foreword by Stephen Shore. -- Shawnee Mission, Kan. :
     Autism Asperger Pub. Co., 2009.

          v. ; cm.

          ISBN: 978-1-934575-40-6
          LCCN: 2009933624

          Summary: A curriculum (consisting of teacher manual and
     student workbooks) to teach and practice self-advocacy skills for
     students with autism spectrum and related disorders. Specifically
     designed for middle- and high-school-aged students, young adults
     in transition, and adults with high-functioning autism and related
     conditions, it includes adaptation ideas for elementary-school
     students and other disability groups.

          1. Autism spectrum disorders--Treatment. 2. Autism--
     Treatment. 3. Asperger's syndrome--Patients--Treatment.
     4. Autistic youth--Education--Study and teaching. 5. Self-help
     techniques. 6. Teachers of children with disabilities--Handbooks,
     manuals, etc. 7. Parents of autistic children--Handbooks, manuals,
     etc. I. Title.

RC553.A88 P37 2009
616.85/88206--dc22   0909

This book is designed in Helvetica Neue and Impact.

Printed in the United States of America.

Table of Contents

Foreword

What if you need to move your desk or workstation from the distraction of the clanging ventilation system or noisy copy machine? Or, suppose the flickering lights over your chair in class keep you from concentrating on the course material? Alternatively, how do you approach your teacher or professor, if you are having trouble keeping up with her lectures because you just can't write fast enough? What if someone had smoked in your "nonsmoking" hotel room before you checked in? What do you do when people look at you from the sides of their eyes after telling a joke that you don't understand?

All of these situations call for some form of self-advocacy. In meeting challenges like those mentioned above, many people simply ask if they can be relocated away from distractions, or they request a copy of the instructor's notes for a fast-paced class. How difficult could it be to tell the jokesters in your life that, while you realize that much of what they say is probably very humorous, you happen to be a very literal type of person and, therefore, don't always "get" their jokes? Likewise, shouldn't it be a snap to simply return to the hotel desk to ask for a different room in which, hopefully, no one has smoked?

For most people the answer is "yes" to all of these self-advocacy-related questions. However, for people on the autism spectrum, rather than learning self-advocacy by observation or osmosis, things are often very different. Just as we need direct support in learning social skills or deciphering nonverbal communication, most of us on the autism spectrum need instruction in learning how to advocate on our own behalf.

Building on *Ask and Tell: Self-Advocacy and Disclosure for People on the Autism Spectrum* (AAPC, 2004) and several other works, Valerie Paradiz has created the first complete curriculum devoted to educating people on the autism spectrum (and, by extension, others with disabilities) to advocate on their own. The *Integrated Self-Advocacy ISA™ Curriculum* is comprised of a teacher's manual and a student workbook, specifically designed for middle and high school students, as well as young adults continuing on after graduation into adulthood. What's more, the Self-Advocacy Portfolio, which is a culminating product of the process, is constructed to fulfill planning requirements for successful transition and documentation for the Individualized Education Program (IEP) or the Individualized Service Plan (ISP).

In units ranging in topic from "What Is Self-Advocacy?" to "Autism in the Media," to "Fostering Our Deep and Focused Interests" and "Exploring Our Role Models," the curriculum guides individuals through exercises that lead to self-discovery. Along the way, they also begin to see more clearly where their strengths and challenges lie. For example, many on the autism spectrum lack sufficient self-awareness to realize that they have sensitivities to stimuli such as fluorescent lights, that they have motor control challenges (which in turn explain their difficulty writing fast enough to keep up with a long string of verbal instructions), or that understanding jokes and idioms is difficult due to their literal conception of language.

Developing this greater self-awareness is critical to understanding the advocacy process. The curriculum guides individuals further, through three important stages that often characterize the act of self-advocacy. First, a student learns how to scan for possible challenges in his or her social and sensory environments. For example, when walking into a restaurant, I scan the environment for the presence of down lights and excess noise with a plan to steer away from these areas, or perhaps even consider a different place to have a meal. (Down lights are lighting fixtures that are embedded in what looks like upside-down coffee cans inserted into the ceiling, creating an unbearable glare similar to looking into a spotlight for many of us on the autism spectrum.) However, should I end up located under a down light,A or if a group of loud diners move next to where I am seated, step two, or creating the advocacy plan, takes place.

This second step focuses on how I plan to explain my need for relocating and thereby develop greater mutual understanding with others of my needs. In this instance, I must also plan whether or not I need to disclose my status as an individual on the spectrum. The decision to make a *full* or *partial* disclosure is a delicate matter, and it is discussed thoroughly in the *Integrated Self-Advocacy ISA Curriculum*. In my particular case in the restaurant, a *partial* disclosure is called for. In other words, I only reveal one specific aspect of being on the autism spectrum as my reason to request a change. In other cases, a *full* disclosure, when I inform others outright that I am on the autism spectrum, may be more appropriate.

My *partial* disclosure can be accompanied by a script that I can think through or even write out in advance, if I need to. My script might run something like: "These lights hurt because I have sensitive eyes" or "These lights give me a headache." Or, if the reason for moving is due to noise, I may mention that I have a difficult time hearing a conversation amidst a lot of background noise.

Finally, in step three, *advocacy* is initiated. This is when I implement my advocacy plan and actually ask the waiter if I might move to a quieter location, or as an alternative, I might ask others I am dining with if they would mind swapping seats with me – given that the down lights don't bother them. If I need to, I can turn to my scripts to make these requests.

The procedure and actions I have described above may seem simple or obvious, and for many, they don't even merit a second thought. However, the process of scanning the environment, developing a plan (including considering disclosure), and then advocating often does not come naturally to many people on the autism spectrum. It took me much thought, along with a lot of trial and error, over many years before I gained the ability to successfully advocate for myself, and the same holds true for many others with autism. The end result is increased self-confidence, comfort, happiness, and overall success.

Another very useful aspect of the *Integrated Self-Advocacy ISA Curriculum* is that many of the units can be adapted for empowering persons with limited or no verbal communication skills to advocate on their own behalves as well. Be sure to keep an eye out for helpful suggestions for adapting the curriculum offered throughout the Teacher's Edition.

In closing, the *Integrated Self-Advocacy ISA Curriculum* has my highest recommendation for those of us on the autism spectrum, as well as for educators, therapists, mentors, coaches, support providers, parents, and other family members of persons with autism. I wish this comprehensive, spot-on curriculum had been available when I was in the early stages of learning how to advocate for myself.

Stephen M. Shore, Ed.D.
Assistant Professor of Education, Ruth S. Ammon School of Education,
Adelphi University, Internationally known author, consultant, and presenter,
board of directors for the Autism Society of America, The Asperger's Association
of New England, and the Advocates for High-Functioning Autism

Introduction

The Integrated Self-Advocacy ISA Curriculum

Welcome to cutting-edge education! You are joining the rising number of professionals, teachers, and families who understand the significance of supporting the emerging self-advocate with autism spectrum disorders (ASD).

If you work at an agency that is striving to create programs and services guided by the principles of person-centered planning, you've turned to the right resource. If your educational team is committed to developing real-world transition plans for older students with autism, or if you're a teacher or therapist wanting to provide curriculum for developing greater autonomy in self-regulation, decision-making, problem-solving, vocational planning, and independent skills, you've come to the right place.

Finally, if you're a family member of a person with autism wishing to "walk the talk" of self-determination in your own home by actively fostering your child's sense of autonomy and responsibility, you will find the materials you need here.

The Integrated Self-Advocacy ISA Curriculum is specifically designed for middle- and high school-aged students, young adults in transition, and adults with high-functioning autism, Asperger Syndrome, and related conditions.

You will also find that most units of the curriculum can be easily adapted for elementary-school students, nonverbal and partially verbal individuals on the spectrum, and other disability groups.

Wherever you see this icon ⟳, you'll find helpful ideas for modifying the lessons for these groups. Additional suggestions for adapting the curriculum to different types of classrooms, small groups, or 1:1 work may be found on page 133 of the Appendix.

First Steps

In school, agency, and home environments, children and adults with ASD often receive limited support in understanding their condition. This is because, as support people, we have little time to develop thoughtful, person-centered materials and tools, or we simply have no clue how to begin to provide this support. And yet, as each day goes by, we are all too aware of our hesitancy to take the first step.

Quite often that first step means dealing with the elephant in the room: sharing the diagnosis. ASD expert Dr. Tony Attwood urges professionals and families to disclose the diagnosis to individuals on the spectrum, inasmuch as it is possible to do so:

> *Clinical experience indicates that it is extremely important that the diagnosis is explained as soon as possible and preferably before inappropriate compensatory mechanisms are developed. The child is then more likely to achieve self-acceptance, without unfair comparisons with other children, and be less likely to develop signs of an anxiety disorder, depression or conduct disorder.*
> (*The Complete Guide to Asperger's Syndrome.* [2007]. London & Philadelphia: JKP; p. 330)

Knowing the diagnosis, however, is only the beginning in learning to advocate for one's needs and preferences independently and effectively. Once we get past the elephant, we discover that we have opened the door to a wealth of advocacy goals and possibilities, which in some cases can even be a bit overwhelming. This is where the ISA curriculum comes in.

The Curriculum

The Integrated Self-Advocacy ISA Curriculum helps us, as professionals and family members, to provide children and adults with ASD with safe forums for self-discovery, structured learning activities, and a cumulative understanding of the many facets of self-advocacy. The 11 units included in the Teacher Edition and Student Workbook provide a comprehensive curriculum with detailed lesson plans, worksheets, and activities, including scanning sensory and social environments, identifying how and when to self-disclose, exploring the history of autism, studying role models with ASD, developing media literacy on topics involving autism, and cultivating deep and focused interests for vocation and leisure time.

If you stop to think about it, self-advocacy plays a vital role in nearly every aspect of life for an individual on the spectrum – in school, at home, in the community, and at work. The more self-aware people on the spectrum become, the more they can be players in advocating for their own comfort, happiness, and well-being.

However, becoming a self-advocate doesn't happen in a vacuum. People with ASD and related conditions of all ages need integrated support to learn the necessary skills. If we want them to become more independent in terms of self-regulation or more aware of themselves when it comes to perspective-taking or understanding the complexities of attribution, we must work together to create genuine opportunities for testing out and experiencing self-reliance, even if it means that those we support make some mistakes along the way.

The good news is we don't need to reinvent the wheel to offer this support. For nearly 15 years, adults with ASD have been hard at work establishing a network of organizations and peer support groups devoted to articulating autistic experience, sharing advocacy strategies, practicing self-disclosure, understanding their legal rights, and developing plans and agendas for change. Such groups include Autism Network International (www.autreat.com), the Global Regional Asperger Syndrome Partnership (www.grasp.org), the Autistic Self-Advocacy Network (www.autisticadvocacy.org), the Autism National Committee (www.autcom.org), and Wrong Planet (www.wrongplanet.net).

This curriculum derives its inspiration and educational philosophy from these pioneers, who have taught us that possessing skills in self-advocacy is as essential as developing better social thinking and social self-awareness (sometimes referred to as "social skills").

Supporting the Disability Movement

As you follow the lesson plans in this book, or write your own using the templates provided, you will become sensitized – along with your students, clients, and loved ones on the autism spectrum – to important trends and issues within the greater disability movement. Imagine yourself being on the forefront of supporting someone in the deaf community, just as that advocacy group was beginning to assert itself in the 1980s and 1990s in debates on whether to use sign language or to learn to speak. The outcome of the deaf community's rigor in advocacy was to provide individuals with choices and the tools and information they needed to make choices. Similarly, you are poised to assist individuals on the autism spectrum in creating a voice for themselves and making disability history.

As educators, professionals, and family members, we must learn to identify when to step back from our training, our know-how, or our paternal and maternal concerns to allow the individual with autism to discover his or her path to personal advocacy. The lessons contained in this book serve two purposes. As we offer support, we are also asked to rethink our approach to teaching and providing therapy. We are invited to not assume we know all the answers and to replace our assumptions with the trust that, by providing them tools and information, our students, clients, and loved ones will seek and discover many solutions themselves.

For example, one unit of the curriculum shows us how to teach individuals with ASD to conduct Sensory Scans™ of environments in order to identify challenges or discomforting elements. Using this information, the person with ASD develops an advocacy action plan to request accommodations or to introduce other strategies to be able to function independently.

Results You Can Expect

In a pilot study in an inner-city school in Manhattan, New York, a nonverbal teenager with hearing challenges, after learning the Sensory Scan™, was able to share with staff that his hearing implement was set too loudly. Until that day, he had not known about the sensory systems, nor had he learned how to identify and communicate his sensory experiences. Without the scan tool, his teachers and family never would have known that this young man was in considerable anguish every day. Once he was able to communicate this discomfort, the hearing device could be calibrated properly, transforming his ability to participate in school.

A Note to School or Agency Administrators

I want this book to be useful to your school or agency. Because this was my ultimate goal in writing it, I must be frank and say to you: According to the Centers for Disease Control and Prevention (http://www.cdc.gov), the current diagnostic rate for individuals on the autism spectrum in the United States is 1 in 150 and rising. For the autistic individuals served[1] by your school or organization, learning skills in self-advocacy will forever change their lives, introducing them to knowledge about themselves that many people with ASD often don't have access to until they are older adults, if at all.

By supporting your teachers, therapists, case managers, and support providers in integrating this curriculum into their classrooms, group and residential settings, and individual counseling or contact sessions, your organization will be providing the infrastructure we so urgently need to support the rising number of individuals diagnosed with autism spectrum conditions.

This curriculum also makes it possible for your educational staff to create responsible, meaningful transition plans that can be shared with families, agencies, and postsecondary institutions. It offers support providers and case managers tools to enhance the Individual Service Plan (ISP) and embrace person-centered thinking. Finally, it includes individuals with autism as important players in shaping their own development as self-advocates.

---

[1]   Throughout the book, I use various ways of describing individuals with autism, including person-first language. I do this because we have discovered, in the self-advocacy community, that we have a variety of preferences for labeling ourselves. As a writer and curriculum developer, I find it best to use the language interchangeably in order to accommodate all.

One word to your staff at a case or faculty meeting can change lives. Speaking highly of autistic students' ability to learn to advocate for their needs can shift the educational ethos of an entire school or agency. By taking these steps, you are participating in how our culture at large imagines people with disabilities. You are opening new doors to every aspect of their quality of life: at work, school, home, and in the community.

How to Use This Curriculum

The Integrated Self-Advocacy ISA Curriculum is designed for a variety of settings in schools and organizations. Here are a few examples:

- Classrooms
- Group or individual counseling
- Social skills class or group
- Therapeutic settings, such as OT or speech/language
- In-home instruction
- After-school or community programs
- ASD programs for college students or young adults
- Residential settings
- Peer support groups
- Mentoring or social coaching
- Transition preparedness

For helpful suggestions on adapting the lesson plans to a variety of classrooms, groups and other settings, look for this icon ⟳. You may also refer to page 133 of the Appendix for more suggestions.

Whenever students see this icon, it's a cue for them to reflect on what they have discovered in a lesson or activity. Reinforcing their insights will help them as they complete their Self-Advocacy Portfolio, and, most important, as they apply their advocacy strategies in real-life situations.

What Is the *Self-Advocacy Portfolio*?

The *Self-Advocacy Portfolio* is the backbone of the Integrated Self-Advocacy ISA system. Unlike the units of the curriculum, the portfolio extends beyond classroom lessons and therapeutic activities into everyday experiences. This is where advocacy learning is translated into practice. Although you will find no lesson plans here, the *Self-Advocacy Portfolio* aims to cover important objectives:

- To provide students with a central location for documenting, reviewing, and updating successful advocacy strategies
- To validate students' development in a format that can be shared with friends, family, mentors, support people, professionals, therapists, employers, physicians, and teachers
- To serve as a living document that has the capacity and flexibility to accompany the individual with autism through a variety of settings and life changes
- To provide helpful information to schools and other state and federal programs that wish to document progress on goals, fortify the IEP or ISP, author meaningful transition plans, or provide evidence for best practices.

Wherever students see this icon ⬙, they will know it is a cue to transfer or translate information they have discovered in a lesson or activity to the **Self-Advocacy Portfolio.** *For more specific information about the portfolio, see pages 109-112.*

Whenever students see this icon, it's a cue for them to think of ways to practice their skills as advocates in their community, or to submit articles or other media they have produced to the Integrated Self-Advocacy ISA web site (www.valerieparadiz.com/community).

A Word of Introduction from the Author, Valerie Paradiz, Ph.D.

I am an individual diagnosed with Asperger Syndrome. I'm also a parent of a son with autism, and I have worked in the field of education as a college professor, teacher, school administrator, and educational consultant for over 20 years. As you implement and adapt the curriculum and lesson plans in this book, I invite you to keep this in mind: In spite of our good training or highly developed insight into our students, clients, and loved ones with autism, we cannot assume that we know what it is like to be in their shoes, to live their sensory lives, or to feel social experiences the way they do. We cannot assume that we always know what might constitute an improvement in quality of life for an individual. We must learn to trust that they themselves, if given the training, opportunity and permission to do so, will open doors of understanding to us that we never imagined.

Welcome! I'm happy you're committed to supporting individuals with ASD in pursuing and realizing the governing principles of self-determination: freedom, authority, autonomy, and responsibility. We need you, and we're glad you're here with us, sharing the journey.

The Integrated Self-Advocacy ISA Curriculum and Lesson Plans

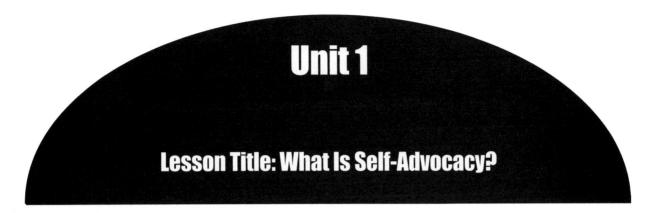

Unit 1

Lesson Title: What Is Self-Advocacy?

Learning Objectives

- To introduce students to the basic concept of self-advocacy
- To learn about self-advocacy through examples
- To begin to explore the significance of partial and full disclosure

Brief Description of Lesson

In this introductory unit, students are introduced to the basic concept of self-advocacy, including the importance of self-disclosure. As students move through the curriculum, these concepts will deepen in meaning. The expanded lesson includes a crossword puzzle to reinforce key ideas and vocabulary.

Materials and Other Instructional Needs

- Whiteboard

A. What Is Self-Advocacy?

1. Have students take turns reading aloud from "What Is Self-Advocacy?" in their Student Workbooks.

2. If needed, have students reread the text silently and highlight unknown vocabulary and words or phrases they wish to discuss.

3. Ask students to write unknown vocabulary words on the board. Ask for definitions or supply them as needed, and write them on the board for visual support.

4. Lead a discussion, reinforcing the self-advocacy goals of this lesson.

 Questions you can ask are also listed in the Self-Reflection section of the Student Workbook:

    a. Have you ever advocated for yourself? Tell the story. What was the outcome?

    b. Have you ever heard or watched your mom, dad, or other family member advocate for you? Tell the story. What was the outcome? Do you think you could have advocated for yourself in this situation, if you had had the words and tools to do so?

What Is Self-Advocacy?
A Word from the Author

My name is Valerie Paradiz, and I am an individual diagnosed with Asperger Syndrome (AS). I didn't know I had AS until I was evaluated at age 40. Imagine what that must have been like! I can tell you it wasn't always easy, but I can also tell you that knowing the diagnosis, even if it's difficult to understand or accept at times, is so much better than NOT knowing. You are, as they say, *ahead of the game* for knowing you have autism or AS. I wrote this book for you, hoping it would give you opportunities to learn more about yourself and to have the ability to take charge of many important aspects of your life!

I'm also the mom of a young man who has autism. His name is Elijah. Sometimes he calls himself "Mr. Inevitable," when he's performing standup comedy on stage. Elijah's jokes are hilarious, and sometimes he even makes fun of being autistic. He also makes fun of special ed. teachers and psychologists and, well, even me, but in a lighthearted way that makes me laugh. I like that about Elijah. Over the years, he has been able to accept his autism and to develop his strengths through his deep interests in performance and music. Elijah is about to go to college now, but ever since he was diagnosed with autism at age 3, we have been on a journey together, the journey of self-advocacy.

Do you know what self-advocacy is? If you know what it is, can you think of a time in your life when you advocated for yourself? If you don't know what it is, you probably have practiced self-advocacy without even realizing it! The purpose of this book is to assist you in becoming a self-advocate, or to get even better at it.

So, where do we begin? Maybe it's best to back up a bit and understand what *advocacy* means in general. Our parents, teachers, and the professionals who support us sometimes advocate for us; they actively speak out on our behalf to assist in improving our quality of life. For example, a father attending a meeting at his son's school asked the teachers and administrators if they would provide special support for his son. His request was to have his son's desk moved closer to the window where there was more natural light.

What the heck? you might ask. That's a strange thing to ask for, but quite often that is the trick of advocacy. The advocate must not only ask for the support, sometimes he must educate those he is making the request of at the same time. The man was asking for this accommodation in the classroom because his son was sensitive to the fluorescent lights. The boy could actually see the flicker of the lights, something that many people don't perceive at all. This was making him cranky and fatigued. It also interrupted his ability to concentrate or participate fully in school. Once the father spoke up – or advocated – for his son's needs, the school was very happy to move his desk near the window, and he was better able to function in the classroom.

Let's take this example a step further. What would a *self*-advocate do in this situation? The self-advocate would be the boy himself. He would be the one to make the request to have his desk moved, rather than his father stepping in to do so. In many instances, teachers might not be open to such suggestions, often because they don't understand that individuals on the autism spectrum experience all sorts of sensory sensitivities – such as the boy's sensitivity to fluorescent lighting. Many of us on the spectrum don't have the tools to self-advocate, and we might end up feeling lost and frustrated about not being supported properly. We might have meltdowns, outbursts, or just plain shut down altogether. But this is no way to live our lives! To be a self-advocate, the boy would have the tools and strategies to be able to make the same request his father made, but he would be able to do it independently and effectively, in the very moment the accommodation is most needed.

I wrote this book so that you would have the chance to learn how to be a self-advocate anywhere you go: out in the community, at home, at work, in school, at the college you attend, or the residence or agency you spend a lot of time at. I also wrote this book so that your teachers, therapists, family members, support people, and the professionals who you regularly see will learn more about autism and discover that self-advocacy is an important part of each day for you.

My son Elijah and I have benefited greatly from learning how to be self-advocates, and we hope that you will, too! You are embarking on an exciting journey, joining other self-advocates with autism across the country and the world! Welcome! Come as you are!

SELF-ADVOCACY New Vocabulary and Ideas	
Words or Phrases	**Definitions and Notes**
1.	1.
2.	2.
3.	3.
4.	4.
5.	5.

B. What Is Disclosure?

1. Have students take turns reading aloud from "What Is Disclosure?" in their Student Workbooks.

2. If needed, ask students to reread the text silently and highlight unknown vocabulary and words or phrases they wish to discuss.

3. Ask students to write unknown vocabulary words on the board. Ask for definitions or supply them as needed, and write them on the board for visual support.

4. Lead a discussion to reinforce the self-advocacy goals of this lesson.

    Questions you can ask are also listed in the Self-Reflection section of the Student Workbook:
   a. Have you ever self-disclosed? Why did you do it? What did it feel like? Tell the story. What was the outcome?
   b. Can you think of examples in your own life where a full disclosure might have worked well for you?
   c. Can you think of examples in your own life where a partial disclosure might have been a good thing to do?
   d. Has anyone you know ever disclosed your autism or Asperger Syndrome without your permission or knowledge? How did this make you feel? Has anyone ever disclosed your diagnosis while you were present? How did this make you feel?

5. To wrap up the exercise, ask students to read Stephen Shore's commentary and pointers on the art of disclosure in "A Few Thoughts on Disclosure." Dr. Shore, like the author of this book, is an individual on the autism spectrum.

What Is Disclosure?

One very important aspect of self-advocacy is disclosure. Disclosure involves telling someone that you have autism or Asperger Syndrome. This can be a very risky or scary thing to do. And sometimes it's not clear whether or not you should reveal this about yourself. I once disclosed my AS at a job interview, and the employer told me (even though it was illegal) that they wouldn't hire me because of my autism. The nerve! I now know that I should have waited to share my diagnosis until it was clearly safe to do so. On the other hand, there are many instances where it is important and even necessary to self-disclose.

A friend of mine who has Asperger Syndrome becomes nonverbal (she cannot speak) when she gets very stressed. This can become a safety issue in an emergency situation, and it can cause misunderstandings. To solve the problem, she carries a laminated card with her at all times. The card has printed messages on it and lets whoever reads it know that she has AS and is unable to speak in the moment. It also lets the reader know that she needs assistance. Contact numbers and other information are included on the card, so that she can seek assistance in an emergency.

There are two types of disclosure: full disclosure and partial disclosure.

In the example above, my friend gave *full disclosure* of her autism, because her laminated card states: "I have autism." But there are some situations when it might not be a good idea to fully disclose and to only offer a *partial disclosure*. For example, a woman on the spectrum once interviewed for a job. She knew that, according to the law, she was not obligated to disclose her autism during her job interview. However, she wanted her interviewer to know that she needed some accommodations on the job. So she disclosed partially by saying that she had a "communication disorder" and that she had strategies for addressing it.

This was a good idea, because the woman knew that she has slow, monotone speech with little inflection. This sometimes causes others to make assumptions like: she's bored, she's depressed, or if you can believe it, she's on drugs! So, by offering a partial disclosure during her job interview, she gave the interviewing committee an explanation for her unusual speech, yet also began the process of advocating for her needs. Later, she was offered the job and was able to disclose fully. Once she disclosed her Asperger Syndrome, she could also educate her coworkers about her communication needs and ask for accommodations at work.

Another way to disclose is to ask someone to do it for you. This can be a helpful solution in some situations, but it is always good to assess whether or not this is the approach that you want to take. To decide, ask yourself, Can I do it myself? Or, if it feels risky, can I ask a friend to be nearby as I do it myself?

Sometimes we find ourselves in the position where someone discloses our diagnosis to others without our knowledge or without asking our permission. They may even disclose this information while we are present. If this has ever happened to you, think about how it made you feel. It can be helpful to pay attention to such situations, in case you wish to have more control over your privacy.

Each time you advocate for yourself, you will be faced with the decision as to whether you should self-disclose or not, or whether you would like to ask someone to do it for you or with you. Each time you will also need to assess whether you wish to make a full or a partial disclosure. Remember, every moment of self-advocacy is unique and requires an original approach to finding the best solution. Once you get the hang of it, however, you'll find that you get better at making these important choices more quickly. And that is why we are discussing and practicing it here.

DISCLOSURE New Vocabulary and Ideas	
Words or Phrases	**Definitions and Notes**
1.	1.
2.	2.
3.	3.
4.	4.
5.	5.

C. A Few Thoughts on Disclosure

A Few Thoughts on Disclosure
Contributed by Stephen Shore, Ed.D.

As mentioned earlier, an important consideration is *how much* you are going to tell. Stating that you have Asperger Syndrome or autism would be considered a *full* disclosure. However, you may decide its better to make a *partial* disclosure. An example might be that your sensitive hearing makes it difficult to concentrate while sitting next to the noisy ventilation system. Often a *partial* disclosure is sufficient.

Finally, script out what you are going to say. (You will learn helpful tools for doing just this in Unit 3.) Writing it out is a technique that works well for many people. Others may be more productive by speaking their thoughts into a recorder, drawing pictures, etc. The choice is yours.

Each advocacy situation is different. It may turn out that you decide that advocacy is not appropriate for a given situation, and that is fine. What is important is that you understand the underlying issues that are giving rise to the potential need to advocate.

 Sometimes it is helpful to disclose prior to reaching the advocacy stage. You will then be working from a position of strength!

 When deciding whether to disclose or not, ask yourself the question, "Does the effect of being on the autism spectrum significantly impact the situation or relationship and is there a need for greater mutual understanding?"

D. Extended Lesson: Crossword Puzzle

Across

1. A modification in actions or in the environment in response to the needs of others

2. Relating to sensation and the sense organs (sight, hearing, taste, etc.)

3. Political or personal independence

4. Incomplete or only a portion of

Down

1. Active verbal (or other form of communication) for a cause or position

5. The identifying of an illness or disorder through an evaluation or tests

6. The revealing of information that was previously private or secret

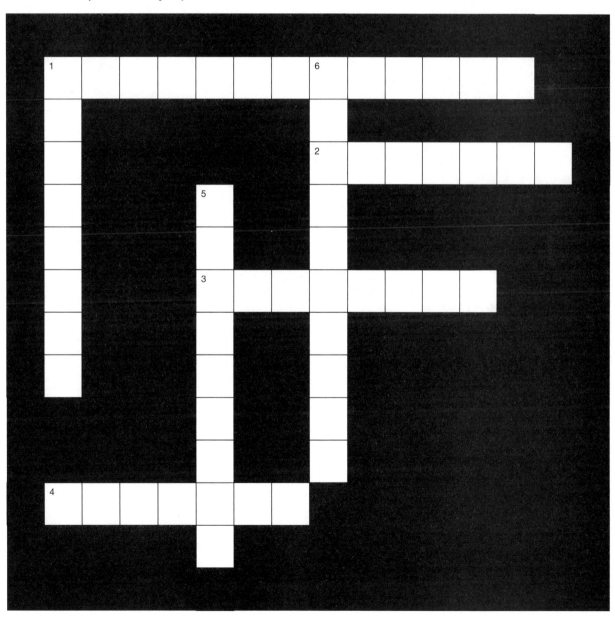

Answer Key:

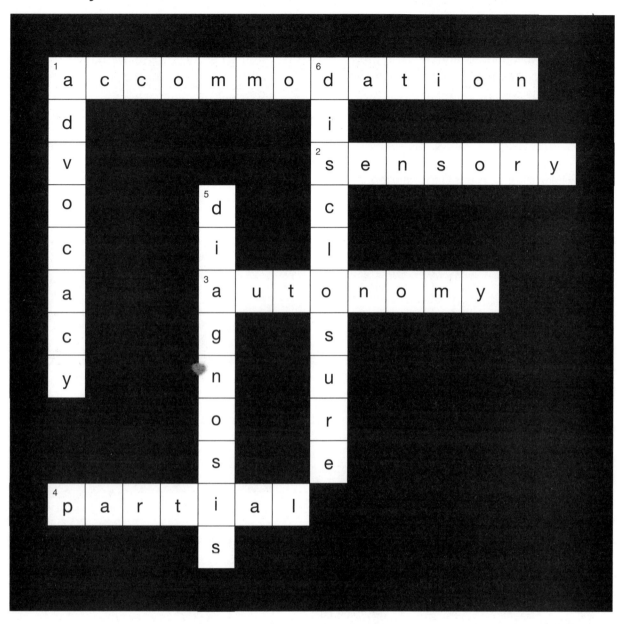

Unit 2

Lesson Title: The Autism Community

Learning Objectives

- To familiarize students with the "autism community"
- To teach the concept of perspectives on autism (individual, family, professional, etc.)
- To validate the autistic perspective as a critical part of the autism community
- To support students in navigating the complexities of attribution

Brief Description of Lesson

Reading brief passages from the professional literature (therapeutic, medical, educational, psychiatric), as well as from parent memoirs, students begin to understand that "autism" is not a static diagnosis or condition and that different people have different perspectives on what autism is. After these readings, students are introduced to brief passages, this time written by individuals with ASD. The exercise helps students see that their own perspectives on autism are necessary and valuable to our community.

Materials and Other Instructional Needs

- Internet access
- Whiteboard

A. The Autism Community

There are many different perspectives on what autism is. Together, all of these perspectives make up what we call the "autism community." In this exercise, students begin to see that, like their teachers, their parents, and the professionals who support them, they, too, have a legitimate voice in the autism community.

1. Have students take turns reading excerpted texts aloud or silently, depending upon class size and student ability.

2. Before beginning each excerpt, point out that this is an "occupational therapist (OT) perspective" or a "psychiatric perspective," etc., and that it is different from other perspectives because it views the individual with ASD in a particular way.

3. If necessary, have students reread the text silently and highlight unknown vocabulary words or phrases they wish to discuss.

4. After students have had enough time to read (and highlight important information), lead a brief discussion on each passage. Solicit information from students on what they know about each of the professions or perspectives represented by the passages.

5. Ask students to write unknown vocabulary words on the board. Ask for definitions or supply them as needed. Write them on the board for visual support.

6. Transition to the next set of quoted passages, written by individuals with ASD. Emphasize that along with the professional, educational, and family perspectives, the *autistic* perspective is another voice (or group of voices) that is important in shaping and contributing to the autism community, including those of the students themselves!

7. Read passages written by individuals with autism. Have students take turns reading excerpted text aloud or silently, depending upon class size and student needs.

8. If necessary, have students reread the text silently and highlight unknown vocabulary words or phrases they wish to discuss.

9. After students have been given enough time to read (and highlight), lead a brief discussion on each passage.

10. Ask students to write unknown vocabulary words on the board. Ask for definitions or supply them as needed. Write them on the board for visual support.

11. In the discussion, reinforce the self-advocacy goals of this lesson. Questions you might ask are listed below and included in the Self-Reflection section of the Student Workbook.

    a. Why is it important for the autism community to hear the autistic perspective?

    b. Why is it important for you to begin to develop your own perspectives?

    c. Can perspectives overlap in agreement or compete and conflict with one another? What strategies can we use to accept this – that there are many perspectives in our community and we need not agree with them all, but we must be able to accept that they are there?

 To offer students visual aids, screen YouTube or other video clips available on the Internet in place of some of the textual quotations above.

Perspectives on Autism and Asperger Syndrome

Child Psychiatry

During the first year of life there may have been a lack of the normal interest and pleasure in human company that should be present from birth. Babbling may have been limited in quantity and quality. The child may not have drawn attention to things going on around him in order to share the interest with other people. He may not have brought his toys to show to his parents or visitors when he began to walk. In general, there is a lack of the intense urge to communicate in babble, gesture, movement, smiles, laughter and eventually speech.

> Lorna Wing, Asperger syndrome: A clinical account, *Psychological Medicine, 11* (1981): 115-129.

Occupational Therapy: Sensory Integration

Sensory integration is the organization of sensations for use. Our senses give us information about the physical conditions of our body and the environment around us. [...] The brain must organize all of these sensations if a person is to move and learn and behave in a productive manner. The brain locates, sorts and orders sensations – somewhat as a traffic officer directs moving cars. When sensations flow in a well-organized or integrated manner, the brain can use those sensations to form perception, behavior and learning. When the flow of sensations is disorganized, life can be like a rush hour traffic jam.

> A. Jean Ayres, *Sensory Integration and the Child* (Los Angeles: Western Psychological Services, 2005), 5.

Parents

Elijah walks in circles all around the house. He doesn't turn his head if someone calls his name. We've had his hearing checked, but everything's in order. He's just a late talker. He's just independent. He wants to climb on windowsills and gaze wordlessly through glass. He wants to peel crayons and line them up in rows or play the threshold game and hide behind the door. Open the door, close the door, peek at mommy through the crack. He hasn't called me "mommy" yet. He's just a late talker. He says only the little words, the monosyllable. "Sad, sad, sad, sad." All day long. Or "fun, fun, fun," looking through the glass.

> Valerie Paradiz, *Elijah's Cup: A Family's Journey into the Community and Culture of High Functioning Autism and Asperger Syndrome* (London: Jessica Kingsley Publishers, 2005), 16.

Teachers: Special Education

Without seeing a visual schedule students [with ASD often] don't know the daily routine. In and of itself, this would not be problematic if [they] were comfortable with "going with the flow" or participating in unplanned activities. But they are not! Activities that seem unpredictable easily cause anxiety, which can lead to problem behavior and lower performance. To help students cope, visual supports have proven very effective. These can be lists of activities to complete, books to take to class, and reminders of what to discuss with peers at lunch.

Brenda Smith Myles, Diane Adreon and Dena Gitlitz, *Simple Strategies That Work! Helpful Hints for All Educators of Students with Asperger Syndrome, High-Functioning Autism, and Related Disabilities* (Shawnee Mission, KS: Autism Asperger Publishing Company, 2006), 20.

Anthropology

[N]o single factor seems to account for the rise [in diagnoses of autism]. Nor should any single factor be accepted at face value. For example, if we accept that scientists are counting cases more accurately than before, we should look into how and why they started counting them better. If we accept that new diagnostic criteria are responsible for the increase in prevalence rates, how and why did the new diagnostic criteria emerge at this time in our history? And if we believe that autism awareness is at an all-time high, how did this happen?

Roy Richard Grinker, *Unstrange Minds: Remapping the World of Autism* (New York: Basic Books, 2006), 10.

Perspectives from Individuals on the Autism Spectrum

Temple Grandin

I think in pictures. Words are like a second language to me. I translate both spoken and written words into full-color movies, complete with sound, which run like a VCR tape in my head. When somebody speaks to me, his words are instantly translated into pictures. Language-based thinkers often find this phenomenon difficult to understand, but in my job as an equipment designer for the livestock industry, visual thinking is a tremendous advantage.

Visual thinking has enabled me to build entire systems in my imagination. During my career I have designed all kinds of equipment, ranging from corrals for handling cattle on ranches to systems for handling cattle and hogs during veterinary procedures and slaughter. I have worked for many major livestock companies. In fact, one third of the cattle and hogs in the United States are handled in equipment I have designed. Some of the people I've worked for don't even know that their systems were designed by someone with autism. I value my ability to think visually, and I would never want to lose it.

Temple Grandin, *Thinking in Pictures, Expanded Edition: My Life with Autism* (New York: Vintage, 2006), 3.

Daniel Tammet

I was born on January 31, 1979 – a Wednesday. I know it was a Wednesday, because the date is blue in my mind and Wednesdays are always blue, like the number 9 or the sound of loud voices arguing. I like my birth date, because of the way I'm able to visualize most of the numbers in it as smooth and round shapes, similar to pebbles on a beach. That's because they are prime numbers: 31, 19, 197, 97, 79 and 1979 are all divisible only by themselves and 1. I can recognize every prime up to 9,973 by their "pebble-like" quality. It's just the way my brain works.

Daniel Tammet, *Born on a Blue Day* (New York: Simon and Shuster, 2007), 1.

Luke Jackson

I am not a genius in this area [math] but a lot of AS kids are. It seems to be one thing that you either excel at or you don't. (I suppose that is a silly statement though because that applies to most things in life.)

A lot of kids with AS love Latin, German and definitely information technology (IT). There may be some subjects which are better suited to an AS person's brain but generally speaking, we are not clones and have our own strengths and weaknesses. Despite the film Rain Man, we don't all have these amazing mathematical skills – I wish!

Luke Jackson, *Freaks, Geeks and Asperger Syndrome* (London: Jessica Kingsley Publishers, 2002), 20.

Liane Willey

I used to rely on a "fitting in" trick that is nothing more than a sophisticated form of echolalia. Like a professional mimic I could catch someone else's personality as easily as other people catch a cold. I did this by surveying the group of people I was with, then consciously identifying the person I was most taken in by. I would watch them intently, carefully marking their traits, until almost as easily as if I had turned on a light, I would turn their personality on in me. I can change my mannerisms and my voice and my thoughts until I am confident they match the person I wanted to echo. Of course, I knew what I was doing, and of course, I was somewhat embarrassed by it, but it worked to keep me connected and sometimes that was all that concerned me. It was simply more efficient for me to use the kinds of behaviors other people used, than it was for me to try and create some of my own.

Liane Holliday Willey, *Pretending to Be Normal* (London: Jessica Kingsley Publishers, 1999), 71.

PERSPECTIVES New Vocabulary and Ideas	
Words or Phrases	**Definitions and Notes**
1.	1.
2.	2.
3.	3.
4.	4.
5.	5.

B. Extended Lesson: Internet Scavenger Hunt

1. If necessary, preteach simple Internet search skills using Google. Include support in conducting Google image searches and YouTube searches to enhance learning through visual supports.

2. Assign students to work in small teams or individually, hunting for the people and organizations in the autism community listed on the scavenger hunt worksheet. Once an item is found, students note important information that they may share later in group discussion or small structured discussions with the teacher.

3. If students work in teams, introduce them to key strategies for successful team-work on page 140 in the Appendix. Provide additional support and structure as needed. For example, you can preassign roles or duties to team members.

 If you have a student with graphomotor challenges or dysgraphia, or a student who has not been assessed for these learning issues but often struggles with organizing thoughts while writing, consider offering him/her access to a computer to complete the worksheet. All worksheets are available for this purpose on the CD provided with this book.

Internet Scavenger Hunt: The Autism Community
Integrated Self-Advocacy ISA™

My Personal Information:

Your name: _____   Date: _____

Class: _____

Find the following hunt items by conducting text, image, or video clip searches on the World Wide Web. Make a few notes that you can share with your teacher or class. Think about the perspective on autism each item in the hunt represents and make notes on that, too.

Person/Organization	Type of Find	Notes on Perspective
Tony Attwood	☐ Text ☐ Picture ☐ Video Clip ☐ Audio Clip	
Mr. Inevitable	☐ Text ☐ Picture ☐ Video Clip ☐ Audio Clip	
Autism Society of America (ASA)	☐ Text ☐ Picture ☐ Video Clip ☐ Audio Clip	
Global Regional Asperger Syndrome Partnership (GRASP)	☐ Text ☐ Picture ☐ Video Clip ☐ Audio Clip	
Dan Marino	☐ Text ☐ Picture ☐ Video Clip ☐ Audio Clip	
The Autistic Self-Advocacy Network (ASAN)	☐ Text ☐ Picture ☐ Video Clip ☐ Audio Clip	
Temple Grandin	☐ Text ☐ Picture ☐ Video Clip ☐ Audio Clip	
The Autism Research Institute (ARI)	☐ Text ☐ Picture ☐ Video Clip ☐ Audio Clip	

Unit 3

Lesson Title: Getting Our Words and Thoughts Out

Learning Objectives

- To understand the challenges in discourse (the "to and fro" of conversation) experienced by many individuals with ASD
- To understand the difference between effective and ineffective advocacy strategies and the role attribution plays in this area
- To write and practice Advocacy Scripts for making requests

Brief Description of Lesson

Reading "The Basic Components of Communication," students learn the basic components of discourse and the differences in communication that individuals with ASD can have. Next, students participate in role-playing exercises aimed at identifying their personal needs and preferences. Self-knowledge in this area can help individuals on the spectrum anticipate triggers and circumvent shutdown, thereby playing a more autonomous role in their self-regulation. After practicing both effective and ineffective advocacy scripts, students are led to develop scripts that represent their own needs and preferences using the Making Advocacy Scripts worksheet. The extended lesson is a word search game that reinforces concepts covered in the chapter reading, "The Basic Components of Communication."

 Remember, successful scripts should be transferred to the Self-Advocacy Portfolio, so that students can turn to them for future use or so that support people or family members can review them.

Materials and Other Instructional Needs

- Whiteboard

A. The Basic Components of Communication

Students take turns reading "The Basic Components of Communication" aloud or silently, depending upon class size and student needs. Illustrations that spell out some common examples of discourse are provided for visual learning and reinforcement. Where needed, assist students in defining and understanding new concepts or vocabulary.

The Basic Components of Communication

"Being autistic is like speaking a different language." This is what a school principal on a Lakota Indian reservation in South Dakota once said about a student with autism. She knew this – even though she does not have autism herself – because she speaks two languages, English and Lakota.

However, if you think about communication, there's more to it than simply knowing how to speak a language. For example, the Lakota Indians feel that making eye contact when speaking with others about important matters is disrespectful. In the dominant culture of the United States, on the other hand, eye contact is expected most of the time when we are speaking with others. In fact, it is often perceived as rude, suspicious, or inattentive if we don't make eye contact.

Eye contact is a form of *nonverbal communication*, and it is just as much a part of how we interact with others as speaking words is. Other types of nonverbal communication are gestures or facial expressions.

Professionals who support individuals with ASD sometimes describe us as having challenges in discourse, or the "to and fro" of interacting with others. We are also said to have challenges in what is called Theory of Mind. Theory of Mind is the ability to sense or anticipate what another person is thinking or, in some instances, to realize that another person is having thoughts that are different from our own. Theory of Mind operates like a sliding scale; all humans possess it in varying degrees.

31

All of these challenges in communication that others tell us we have can make us feel worried or misunderstood at times. You might have experienced this feeling yourself. A constructive way to approach our differences in communication is to think of ourselves as meeting others part way, as if we come from another culture and speak a different language. This requires a subtle shift in how you approach interactions with others, but it can be a helpful way to have more successful moments every day and to find effective ways of advocating for your needs and preferences.

Whatever we bring to an interaction, verbally or nonverbally, contributes to the discourse of that scene. Here's an example:

"Asking for the Time"
Analysis: In this discourse, the initiator in this scene is asking another person for the correct time. The responder raises his arm up and replies that he does not know what time it is. He raises his arm as a gesture to show that he is not wearing a watch.

In any given situation, you might be an initiator or a responder. During a longer period of communication, you might even switch roles several times – going from initiator to responder and back again. Many of us on the autism spectrum have a different way of taking on these roles in communication with others. Sometimes we experience delays in processing what others are saying, or we have challenges tracking interaction when more than one person is speaking with us. For this reason, we sometimes don't satisfy or anticipate other people's expectations of us. On the facing page is a common communication misfire that can happen between an individual on the spectrum and another person.

"Saying Goodbye"

Analysis: The initiator in this scene is saying goodbye to someone who is leaving the room. The initiator has a puzzled look on his face (nonverbal communication) because the person leaving didn't let him know he was going to step out. The responder leaves without saying goodbye or looking at the initiator. In this scene, the responder does not appear to hear, or seems distant to the initiator.

In still other situations, people with autism have trouble getting the right words out. Quite often, for example, we don't know how to make an effective request, as in the illustration below.

"It's too Loud in Here!"

Analysis: The initiator has his hands over his ears and is yelling, "It's too loud in here!" The responder, who is surprised because he doesn't think it's very loud in the room, yells back angrily, "What's your problem? Why are you so mad at me?" In this scene, the initiator is more sensitive to the volume of the radio shown in the picture than the responder is. However, the initiator's attempt to get the volume reduced is ineffective because he is yelling, because he has used no gestures (such as pointing at the radio), and because he has surprised the responder.

Think about this scene. Can you write a new, effective script for the initiator in the empty dialogue bubble in the illustration below, one that would cause the responder to understand his needs and turn the radio down?

B. Role Play: Making Requests and Expressing Personal Preferences

 All too often, we educators use the words "appropriate" and "inappropriate" without providing meaningful feedback to enable students to distinguish what is and is not effective language or action in various social settings. As you move through the role-play exercises below, we encourage you to use the words "effective" and "ineffective" rather than "appropriate" and "inappropriate," to avoid placing value judgments on students' attempts at communicating their needs. Also, try to offer specific information on what makes different interactions effective or ineffective.

1. Choose an ineffective communication scene from those offered in the illustrations on the following pages, or sketch your own scene. Share the scene with students by sketching it on the board or passing out handouts.

2. Ask students to enact the ineffective advocacy scene. Have fun hamming it up with them!

3. Analyze the scene with students by identifying responder and initiator, verbal and nonverbal communication. Explore what the underlying thoughts and emotions might be.

4. Ask students to write new, effective scripts for the scene. Model and analyze them as before.

   • "Somebody Stinks in Here!"
      leaving the room because someone is
      wearing perfume (sensory advocacy)

   • "Shut Up! You're annoying me!"
      putting down others in the room,
      without realizing that one needs
      some alone time to self-regulate
      (social advocacy)

   • "Zoning Out"
      while the teacher is giving a
      lecture (OT advocacy)

   • "Where Am I?"
      lost in a large airport, due to
      overstimulation (self-disclosure,
      asking for help)

C. Creating an Advocacy Script

After students complete this segment of the lesson, they will transfer their Advocacy Scripts to their Self-Advocacy Portfolios. The worksheet Making Advocacy Scripts should be used not only for this lesson, but is meant as a tool for future needs. Once an Advocacy Script is written, it should be included in the Self-Advocacy Portfolio, particularly if it is a script a student finds helpful or successful.

1. Ask students to think about a personal preference they would like others to understand better.

2. Using the Making Advocacy Scripts worksheet, students prepare a script they can use for requesting a need or preference. For example, a student who is sensitive to fluorescent lighting can create an advocacy script requesting that the lights be turned off or that she is allowed to sit near a window where there is more natural light.

3. In group settings, students can transfer script illustrations to the whiteboard or pass around their worksheets for others to see.

4. Students can also model and analyze their scripts with classmates, the teacher or therapist.

5. Ask students to transfer their scripts to the *Self-Advocacy Portfolio* on page 88 of the Student Workbook.

Making Advocacy Scripts
Integrated Self-Advocacy ISA™

Your name: _____   Date: _____

My Advocacy Goal, Need, or Preference

Briefly describe the advocacy goal, need, or preference for which you'll be writing a script:

Analyze the Context	Write Your Answers
LOCATION: Where will you be using this script? What is the environment like? Public, private? Will you need to request privacy to say your script?	
WHO? Who will you be saying your script to? Is it one person or more than one person?	
DISCLOSURE: Do you feel you need to self-disclose to reach your advocacy goal? If you do, will you make a full or partial disclosure?	
OUTCOME: What outcome do you hope to achieve using this script? What will you do if the outcome is different from what you expected?	
SUPPORT: Will you ask a support person to be present when you use your advocacy script? Will you ask a support person to follow up with you after you have attempted advocating with your script?	
ADDITIONAL CONSIDERATIONS: Add any additional information that isn't covered above yet is important to using your script.	

Illustrate and Write the Script

Use the space provided below to illustrate and/or write your advocacy script. Be sure to write the words you will say when you advocate for your need or preference.

Illustrate (if you need more space, please use a separate sheet)

Write Your Script Here (keep it simple and courteous)

 Remember, you can offer students the option of using electronic versions of the worksheets and the Self-Advocacy Portfolio provided on the CD that accompanies this book. Many students with autism spectrum and related conditions can perform better when given the option of working on a computer.

Before You Try out Your Script

Remember that every time you advocate for yourself, you are in an original moment in your life. Although you have prepared this script and have imagined how you would like things to go when you use it, remember that you might not get the results you want, or that the words you are prepared to say might come out differently. In any advocacy moment, it's important to keep an open mind and *expect* that things won't always go the way you want them to. Advocacy is an ongoing process. The success is in attempting it!

Follow up and *The Self-Advocacy Portfolio*

After you have used your Advocacy Script, assess how things worked out. Make any revisions you would like to the script, then transfer the revised version to your *Self-Advocacy Portfolio* on page 88.

Assessment

A. On a scale from 1 to 4, how effective was your script in achieving your advocacy goal or need? (Circle one.)

1	2	3	4
The plan backfired or was a total disaster.	The plan went O.K., but I didn't reach my goal.	The plan went O.K., and I only reached part of my goal.	The plan was a success. I reached my goal.

B. If you chose 1 above, do you feel you need to take another approach? If yes, how?

C. If you chose 2 or 3 above, how can you improve your advocacy script? Make any changes here:

Transfer your successful or revised script to the scripts section of your **Self-Advocacy Portfolio on page 88. The portfolio is a living document where you can save helpful advocacy tools that have worked for you.**

D. Extended Lesson: Word Search

Find the words in the list below in vertical, horizontal, or diagonal directions.

Discourse	Theory of Mind	Gesture
Nonverbal	Initiator	Responder
Script	Communication	

```
t  h  e  o  r  y  o  f  m  i  n  d  q  n
i  w  g  v  e  r  s  l  l  b  o  i  u  i
n  b  e  q  s  v  m  w  o  n  n  s  j  k
i  o  s  z  p  b  o  w  y  m  v  c  b  l
t  q  t  c  o  s  k  e  t  k  e  o  e  t
i  g  u  l  n  b  c  t  t  p  r  u  a  q
a  h  r  q  d  m  l  r  r  o  b  r  x  z
t  j  e  g  e  w  u  s  i  y  a  s  c  d
o  m  u  d  r  p  g  d  y  p  l  e  v  t
r  c  o  m  m  u  n  i  c  a  t  i  o  n
```

Answer Key:

```
t  h  e  o  r  y  o  f  m  i  n  d  q  n
i  w  g  v  e  r  s  l  l  b  o  i  u  i
n  b  e  q  s  v  m  w  o  n  n  s  j  k
i  o  s  z  p  b  o  w  y  m  v  c  b  l
t  q  t  c  o  s  k  e  t  k  e  o  e  t
i  g  u  l  n  b  c  t  t  p  r  u  a  q
a  h  r  q  d  m  l  r  r  o  b  r  x  z
t  j  e  g  e  w  u  s  i  y  a  s  c  d
o  m  u  d  r  p  g  d  y  p  l  e  v  t
r  c  o  m  m  u  n  i  c  a  t  i  o  n
```

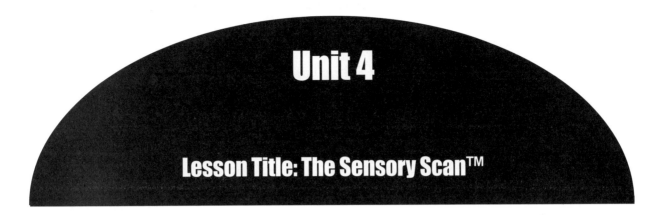

Unit 4

Lesson Title: The Sensory Scan™

Learning Objectives

- To familiarize students with common sensory integration challenges related to ASD
- To teach students how to conduct Sensory Scans at school, at home, and in the community
- To assist students in developing and implementing an Advocacy Plan using the scan data they have collected

Brief Description of Lesson

In this lesson, students are introduced to the basic concepts of sensory integration as they read the essay, "Welcome to the World of Sensory Integration." Many students diagnosed with autism spectrum and related conditions experience hyper- and hyposensitivity, including sensory overwhelm, sensory scrambling, and other types of environmentally related challenges. Quite often, these challenges become obstacles to participation in class, or they may be the source of sudden or chronic problematic behaviors.

Using the Sensory Scan worksheet, students learn how to scan environments as a means of sensitizing themselves to both everyday and novel environments. In this lesson, students conduct their fist scans in the school environment, then at home or in the community. As an extended lesson, they may learn more self-regulation techniques by practicing how to use the Sensory Graphic Equalizer, a visual tool developed by Dr. Stephen Shore, professor of education at Adelphi University, who is also an adult with autism.

After completing Sensory Scans, students develop tools and methods for addressing environmental challenges and triggers by creating their own Advocacy Plan. This is done by transferring important data from the Sensory Scan – "My Top Three Environmental Needs" – to page 91 of the Self-Advocacy Portfolio in the Student Workbook. There, students create plans for becoming more autonomous players in their own self-regulation. Advocacy Plans can be developed any time, as student needs arise at home, school, or in the community.

Materials and Other Instructional Needs

- Whiteboard

A. Sensory Integration and the Sensory Scan

1. Have students take turns reading "Welcome to the World of Sensory Integration" aloud from their Student Workbooks.

2. If needed, have students reread the text silently and highlight unknown vocabulary or phrases they wish to discuss.

3. Copy the Sensory Diagram grid on the whiteboard as it appears on page 45. Students have the identical grid in their Student Workbook. Ask students to assist you in filling in the missing information on the board.

4. Lead a discussion, offering a preliminary exploration of individual sensory experiences, needs, and preferences. If students have trouble articulating their needs, offer some suggestions for each student. This might also be a good moment to explore the topic of attribution and how difficult sensory experiences can affect one's ability to understand the environment or the actions of others.

Questions you might ask are also included in the Self-Reflection section of the Student Workbook:

a. Are you aware of any sensory challenges you have? Loud noises? Background noise? Don't like being touched? Difficulty reading handouts? Trouble with smells, like perfume? Can't feel hot things or other types of pain? Challenge with fluorescent lighting?

b. Have you ever felt frustrated by something in the sensory environment at home, in the community, or at school? Give examples. How did you react to it (got angry, said something that may or may not have been effective or well taken, tried to simply endure)?

c. If you could change one thing in this room in terms of how it pertains to your senses, what would it be and why?

Welcome to the World of Sensory Integration

Since you are a person with an autism spectrum diagnosis or related condition, you, like so many of us with ASD, probably have challenges with the sensory world. Sometimes these challenges are difficult for us auties and aspies to identify, and quite often it's even harder for those around us to see or understand them.

Welcome to the world of sensory integration! The term "sensory integration" was coined by a remarkable woman named Jean Ayres. Dr. Ayres developed a theory that says our senses provide our brains with information about the environment around us, which in turn helps us respond to or organize our activities. For example, if you are indoors in a dark room and then step outside into a very sunny environment, you might find it difficult to adjust to the bright light. With time, your eyes might adapt to the change; however, some of us might need to take additional steps in order to be able to remain outdoors, such as putting on a hat or wearing a pair of sunglasses.

If you think about it, we are constantly informed by sensory experiences. You might have been told that there are five senses, but researchers have actually found that, in addition to the five traditional senses we often hear about (visual, oral [taste], olfactory [smell], tactile [touch], and auditory [hearing]), there are two additional senses that can be less obvious to us. They are called the vestibular and proprioceptive systems. The *vestibular system* involves the position of your head and gravity. It tells you whether you are moving, spinning, or upside down. The *proprioceptive system* involves your awareness of your body, or parts of your body, in space, including your awareness of the direction in which your body is moving and the force with which it is moving.

Many of us on the autism spectrum have challenges with sensory integration. In other words, we don't adjust easily to some environments. For example, we might perceive sounds or smells that don't seem to bother others. At times, they can be so challenging that they prevent us from being able to participate fully in school lessons, activities with our families, or in community events.

The good news is that once you know more about your sensory profile (your sensory needs and preferences), you can either prepare for difficult sensory situations or you can advocate for a modification in the environment. On the following page is a list of all seven sensory systems. See if you can fill in the missing information in the grid – what function the particular sensory system fulfills. Your teacher can assist you with any areas you don't understand completely.

Sensory Diagram		
	Sensory System	**Function**
	Visual	
	Olfactory	
	Oral	
	Auditory	
	Tactile	
	Vestibular	
	Proprioceptive	

B. The Sensory Scan

Using the Sensory Scan worksheet in their workbooks, ask students to scan a room or other environment in the school. They can scan the classroom they are in, and/or, to make the lesson more effective, they may wish to scan areas such as the cafeteria during lunch, the hallways between periods, a general ed. classroom, at work, or in a P.E. class.

The Sensory Scan™ Worksheet
Integrated Self-Advocacy ISA™

My Personal Information & Scan Location

Your name: _____ Date: _____

School/grade/program:_____

Which room or environment will you be scanning? _____

The Sensory Scan

1. **Auditory Scan:** Pay attention to **the sound** in this environment. Which of the following apply to you? Fill in as many details as you can in the Notes sections.

   ☐ Background noise is distracting
   Notes:

   ☐ Challenge with number or volume of voice(s)
   Notes:

   ☐ Sudden loud noises
   Notes:

   ☐ Other
   Notes:

2. **Visual Scan:** Pay attention to **what you see or how you see** in this environment. Which of the following apply to you? Fill in as many details as you can in the Notes sections.

   ☐ Light in room is too bright or too dim
   Notes:

   ☐ Angle of light is difficult (from above, below, etc.)
   Notes:

   ☐ Distracted by things hanging on the wall or in my peripheral vision
   Notes:

   ☐ Type of light is distracting or challenging
   Notes:

   ☐ Challenges reading in this environment
   Notes:

   ☐ Other
   Notes:

3. **Olfactory Scan (Smell):** Pay attention to the **smells** in this environment. Which of the following apply to you? Fill in as many details as you can in the Notes sections.

   ☐ Smell from objects is distracting, challenging
   Notes:

   ☐ Smell from person(s) is distracting, challenging
   Notes:

   ☐ The general smell of the room is difficult
   Notes:

   ☐ Other
   Notes:

4. **Tactile Scan (Touch/Feel):** Pay attention to **your reaction to touch or to the things or people you touch/feel** in this environment. Which of the following apply to you? Fill in as many details as you can in the Notes sections.

   ☐ Generally cannot tolerate others' touch
   Notes:

   ☐ Sometimes don't feel pain the way others do
   Notes:

   ☐ Challenges with how things or surfaces feel to the touch (sticky, wet, rough, etc.)
   Notes:

   ☐ Other
   Notes:

5. **Oral Scan:** Pay attention to **tastes or textures on your tongue** in this environment. Which of the following apply to you? Fill in as many details as you can in the Notes sections.

   ☐ Challenges with the texture or taste of certain foods
   Notes:

   ☐ Challenges with mixed foods
   Notes:

   ☐ Other/Notes:

6. **Vestibular Scan:** Pay attention to **how movement affects or doesn't affect you** in this environment. Which of the following apply to you? Fill in as many details as you can in the Notes sections.

   ☐ Cannot sit for long periods of time
   Notes:

   ☐ Would like to spin in circles
   Notes:

   ☐ Motion in vehicles is disruptive/makes me feel sick or confused
   Notes:

   ☐ Other
   Notes:

7. **Proprioceptive Scan:** Pay attention to your experience of **your body and the space around you**. Which of the following apply to you? Fill in as many details as you can in the notes sections.

   ☐ Easily bump into others or the walls
   Notes:

   ☐ Need to rock, bounce, or press against other things or people
   Notes:

   ☐ Trouble writing on paper (graphomotor)
   Notes:

   ☐ Difficulty using stairs or walking down an incline
   Notes:

   ☐ Cannot sit for long periods of time
   Notes:

   ☐ Other
   Notes:

My Top Three Environmental Needs: Choose up to three results from your Sensory Scan above. You will use these to develop an Advocacy Plan in your *Self-Advocacy Portfolio* on page 91.

   1.

   2.

   3.

Using the information they have gathered from the scan – My Top Three Environmental Needs – students proceed to page 91 of the Self-Advocacy Portfolio to create an Environmental Advocacy Plan that includes strategies for addressing environmental challenges and possibly writing scripts for requesting modifications. The Self-Advocacy Portfolio *is the backbone of* The Integrated Self-Advocacy ISA Curriculum *and serves as a living document of a student's advocacy strategies and tools. Encourage students to use the Sensory Scan worksheet as often as the need arises, and to document any advocacy plans they create in their portfolios.*

We all have a sensory profile, whether we are on the spectrum or not. To make students feel more comfortable doing scans, conduct a Sensory Scan yourself and report on the results you discover. You can carry this a step further by creating your own Advocacy Plan and share it with your students.

Remember, you can offer students the option of using electronic versions of the worksheets and the Self-Advocacy Portfolio provided on the CD that accompanies this book. Many students with autism spectrum and related conditions can perform better when given the option of working on a computer.

C. *Extended Lesson: The Graphic Sensory Equalizer*

1. Ask students to read "The Graphic Sensory Equalizer."
2. After reading the segment, ask students to create their own equalizers and share the results with the group (or with you if you are working 1:1).

The Graphic Sensory Equalizer
A Special Segment Contributed by Stephen Shore, Ed.D.

As we have learned in this unit, there are times when the brain has difficulty managing certain types of information and input, which can result in sensory challenges. When this happens, it is as if some of the senses are turned up too high, causing too much data to come in, whereas other senses may be too low, with not enough data being made available to the brain. Often the data coming are scrambled to some degree. As a result, many people on the autism spectrum depend on unreliable information, which makes it harder to successfully interact with input from the environment.

Everyone has sensory differences. For example, some people turn up the radio or television volume high in order to hear a news broadcast. Others, like myself, keep the volume very low, to a point where some complain they can't hear anything at all. One tool that can help you to understand your own sensory profile in any given situation is the Sensory Graphic Equalizer.

The Sensory Graphic Equalizer

The Graphic Sensory Equalizer above depicts someone's sensory profile. Let's take a look at how this might play out in real life.

The Senses and Sensory Violations

The hypersensitive sense of sight is depicted in the example on page 49 with a slider up to almost positive 10 (+10). This person may be hypersensitive to fluorescent lights, perceiving them as a strobe light. It's also likely that this person has difficulties in the presence of down lights shining from above. Wearing a baseball cap may be helpful in such situations.

Touch is also hypersensitive for this person, but not quite as much as sight, resulting in difficulties in tolerating light touch on the skin (from others) or the feel of certain textures. Hearing is the most sensitive system on this person's equalizer, meaning that the person may perceive sounds such as the electricity in wires, or the buzzing of the ballasts in fluorescent lights may be intolerable. Note that the sense of taste in this case might be considered as "flat" or average, because the slider is at "0."

Moving on, low readings in the vestibular and proprioceptive realms indicate hyposensitivity, resulting in the need to seek sensory input. A person with sliders at this low end may like to spin herself around, seek deep pressure, and may consider a day on a roller coaster as great fun.

Now it is time to fill out your own Sensory Graphic Equalizer. Using the situation where you are currently (the classroom, at home, etc.), simply indicate on the scale of -10 to +10 where you feel your sensory experience is.

My Sensory Equalizer

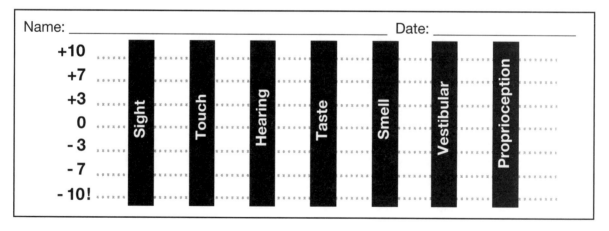

Instructions

1. Mark on the slider where you think your particular senses should be placed. If you are not sure, write your best guess in the form below.

2. In the form below, write something about each of your senses. If you are unable to think of anything at this time, make a check mark to remind you to come back later when something comes to mind.

---

1. Sight _____

   _____

2. Touch _____

   _____

3. Hearing _____

   _____

4. Taste _____

   _____

5. Smell _____

   _____

6. Vestibular _____

   _____

7. Proprioception _____

   _____

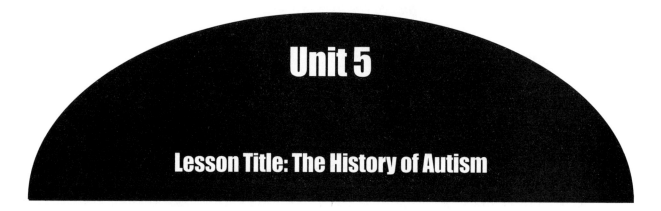

Unit 5

Lesson Title: The History of Autism

Learning Objectives

- To familiarize students with major periods in the history of autism
- To review the concept of multiple perspectives on autism, particularly how these perspectives can change with time (continuation from Unit 2)
- To demonstrate how individuals on the autism spectrum play a role in shaping the history of autism

Brief Description of Lesson

Students read "The History of Autism" provided in their Student Workbooks. The history covers important periods or events in the lives of individuals with ASD, including its "discovery" in the 1940s by Leo Kanner and Hans Asperger and the inclusion of Asperger Syndrome in the *Diagnostic and Statistical Manual of Mental Disorders IV* (DSM IV) in 1994. It also covers current trends in research and thinking about ASD, including the emergence of the neuro-diversity and biomedical communities. As an expanded lesson, students conduct an interview with someone in the autism community.

Materials and Other Instructional Needs

- Whiteboard

A. The History of Autism: Review of Perspectives on Autism

As we learned in Unit 2, there are many different perspectives on what autism is or what it means. Together, all of these perspectives make up what we call the "autism community." In this unit, students begin to see that what we call the "history of autism" is a collection of multiple perspectives that change over time.

1. Ask students to take turns reading "The History of Autism" aloud in their Student Workbooks.

2. If needed, ask students to reread the text silently and highlight unknown vocabulary and words or phrases they wish to discuss.

3. Ask students to write unknown vocabulary words on the board. Ask for definitions or supply them as needed and write them on the board for visual support.

4. Lead a discussion, reinforcing the self-advocacy goals of this lesson.

 Questions you might ask are also included in the Self-Reflection section of the Student Workbook.

   a. Do you think your perspective on autism can shape history? If so, how? If not, why?

   b. Given what you have read, do you think that the lives of people with autism have improved, worsened, or remained the same over time? How did you come to this conclusion?

   c. If you could change one thing in our society today with regard to how it treats or thinks of autistic people, what would it be? How might an advocate go about promoting that change?

The History of Autism

Did you know that autism has a history? It might sound like a strange idea at first, but if you think about it, it makes sense. History is basically how human beings perceive events and document them over time. Most often, in any given era or historical period, the dominant perspective is recorded as being reflective of the culture of the time.

However, there are always minority perspectives that co-exist with the dominant perspective, and sometimes new perspectives emerge, urging us to rethink past events. As you can see, history is very rich and complex. It is ever-changing, as human beings travel together through time and shared events.

For many years, the history of autism was told mainly from psychiatric and medical perspectives. These perspectives were influential in determining the dominant view of what autism was. In those early days (the first half of the 20th century), individuals on the autism spectrum weren't called "autistic." Other terms were used to describe us, some of which seem disrespectful today, such as "idiot savant" or "imbecile."

Then, in the 1940s, two child psychiatrists, Leo Kanner and Hans Asperger, working independently of one another – even in different parts of the world – each identified a condition they observed in children, which they called "autism." Hans Asperger – we would later learn in the 1980s when his research was rediscovered – was identifying children who today would be diagnosed with Asperger Syndrome. As you can see, sometimes a condition is named after the person who first studied or identified it.

"Autism" was an interesting word for Kanner and Asperger to choose. Its root meaning comes from the Greek "autos," meaning "self." For these researchers, the perception was that individuals with autism were locked inside themselves, inaccessible, or "living in their own worlds." We know today that this is not the case. Quite often, when individuals with autism have support in learning communication skills, the distance others sense in us turns out to be more complex than it appears on the surface. We might seem distant because we are coping with sensory or social stresses around us that are invisible to our neurotypical friends, or we might have trouble processing information and responding swiftly in social situations (either verbally or through communication devices), leaving others to think we don't wish to participate. But autism is a way of life, and like any other cultural group, we have our own methods for navigating and being in the world.

As decades went by, theories and practices on how to medically and therapeutically "treat" individuals with autism emerged. By the 1960s and 1970s, Freudian psychology had made its way fully into mainstream therapy, and many professionals working with individuals on the autism spectrum were greatly influenced by its basic premises. Therefore, therapists would "analyze" patients in their care, seeking out associations between their behaviors and how they were raised as children. One common belief at the time was that parents, particularly mothers, were the cause of their children's autism. Some therapists – including a very influential researcher named Bruno Bettelheim – used the phrase "refrigerator mother" to describe women who were so cold and distant as mothers that it caused their children to become autistic. Of course, this approach was not correct and has since been disproved.

In the 1970s and 1980s, parents began to express a stronger voice about how their children were viewed and treated by professionals. One researcher, Bernard Rimland, was a major figure in this new trend and led a parent movement that insisted that professionals incorporate parents' knowledge of their children's needs into practice. Rimland was the father of a child with autism, and his efforts led to important advocacy coalitions among families. One of these became the Autism Society of America (ASA). ASA is the oldest organization devoted to enhancing the lives of individuals on the spectrum, their families, and the professionals who support them. Check out the web site some time: www.autism-society.org. You will find lots of interesting information.

In the 1980s another important development occurred in the research of Dr. Lorna Wing, who first used the phrase "autism spectrum" to describe our way of life. By presenting autism as a range of strengths and challenges, Wing opened new doors to diagnosis and evaluation. Throughout the 1980s, 1990s, and into this century, an array of methodologies and theories about how to support individuals with autism have emerged. Some are medical in nature; others are educational or therapeutic. You might have heard of some of these approaches or philosophies, such as applied behavioral analysis (ABA), Floor Time, biomedical treatment, relationship development intervention (RDI), or the neuro-diversity movement. This is by no means an exhaustive list, but we encourage you to explore the various philosophies, groups, and methods that have emerged.

Probably the most significant development in the history of autism has been the increase in diagnoses of autism in the past 20 years. In the 1980s, estimates of autism in the population were placed at 4 in 10,000 individuals. In 2009, the number is at 1 in 150 and rising according to the Centers for Disease Control and Prevention (http://www.cdc.gov). Historians sometimes refer to sweeping change such as this as *paradigm shifts*. These are large-scale social developments that result in profound change within the mainstream culture. If you think about the advent of the Internet and how different life might have been before it existed, you might have an idea of the magnitude of what is called a "paradigm shift."

A profound shift is happening within the autism community today! Never before have there been so many organizations, both non-profit and for-profit, devoted to autism research, education, and advocacy. In 2006, the Unites States Congress passed the unprecedented Combating Autism Act, which has released funding to schools, hospitals, and other institutions, so that we can begin to understand why there are more people diagnosed with autism than ever before and how we should go about supporting them. Different groups within the autism community have different perspectives on how this funding should be used, and that is why it's a good idea to find out which groups resonate the most with you.

You are alive during an important epoch in autistic history! After the emergence of organized parent advocacy in the 1970s and 1980s, another new voice began to make itself known – the voice of individuals on the spectrum. In the 1990s, the first autistic advocates created peer support groups for individuals on the spectrum and initiated organizations that were devoted to fostering advocacy agendas developed by autistic people. Today we can enjoy such events as Autreat, a yearly retreat planned by autistic people for autistic people, or we can visit web sites like, WrongPlanet.net, which is maintained by a man with Asperger Syndrome. Other groups and organizations include the Global Regional Asperger Syndrome Partnership (GRASP; www.grasp.org) or Autistics United Together And Showing They Indeed Can Succeed (AUTASTICS; www.autastics.org). Other groups you should check out are The Autism National Committee (Autcom; www.autcom.org) and the Autistic Self-Advocacy Network (ASAN; autisticadvocacy.org).

Collaboration with autistic people within established parent and professional organizations has also begun to happen, so that the views and experiences of individuals on the spectrum can reach larger segments of the autism community. For example, in 2007, the Autism Society of America initiated an advisory committee to support its board of directors. Everyone on this special committee has autism! We've come a long way, and you are a part of what is to come, as the history of autism unfolds before us.

HISTORY OF AUTISM New Vocabulary and Ideas	
Words or Phrases	**Definitions and Notes**
1.	1.
2.	2.
3.	3.
4.	4.
5.	5.

B. Extended Lesson: Interview Someone in the Autism Community

1. Have students work as a class, in small groups, or individually.
2. If students work in teams, ask them to review the information on page 59 (in the Student Workbooks, it is on page 41), "Let's Work Together."
3. Next, refer students to the Interview Worksheet on pages 42-43 in their Student Workbooks. This will guide them through a step-by-step process in preparing to conduct an interview.
4. Students can choose to report on their interview orally, visually (PowerPoint® or video), or in writing (or any combination thereof).

 This icon represents places in the curriculum where students are invited to become advocates in their communities, or to submit articles or other media they have produced to the Integrated Self-Advocacy web site.

 Remember, you can offer students the option of using electronic versions of the worksheets and the Self-Advocacy Portfolio provided on the CD that accompanies this book. Many students with autism spectrum and related conditions can perform better when given the option of working on a computer.

Let's Work Together

How to Be an Effective and Supportive Team Member

1. Make sure each of your team members has a clearly defined job to do. If you are not certain what your role is, make sure to get support in defining it.

2. Don't do other members' jobs. Remember, when you work in a team, everyone participates. If you interrupt or offer too much input, others might not be participating as much as they would like to.

3. Make suggestions politely, rather than bossing or telling someone else what to do. When making a suggestion, you can say:

   "I'd like to suggest that we …," or

   "I have another possible way of looking at it …," or

   "What if we were to try …"

   This is how you offer constructive suggestions rather than critical remarks. This is a good thing to practice with your classmates because you need to know how to do team work and cooperate with others in many situations in life.

   Also, when you make a suggestion, always be prepared for various outcomes (rather than what you wish or imagine will happen). For example,

   a) Your suggestion might get adopted by the group.

   b) You suggestion might get turned down.

   c) A portion of your suggestion might be accepted or adapted.

4. Allow the group to vote on decisions that aren't getting unanimous support from each member. Everyone must agree to accept the vote so that you can move on to the next step in the project.

5. Allow all members to process information at their own pace. This shows respect for your fellow classmates.

6. Offer each other positive support. You can say:

   "That's was really terrific how you…," or

   "I like your ideas!" or

   "You're an important part of this project! Thank you!"

7. Don't say critical things to one another, since this only slows down the process and makes others feel unhappy and unable to work as a team.

Interview Worksheet
Integrated Self-Advocacy ISA™

Preparing for the Interview

Your name: _____   Date: _____

Name of interviewee: _____

To interview someone in the autism community, you must first decide whether you wish to (check one):

- ☐ Conduct a verbal interview in person or by phone
- ☐ Conduct a written interview by email or online chat
- ☐ Conduct a video interview in person

What type of report will you make?

- ☐ Article (textual)
- ☐ Oral presentation (verbal)
- ☐ PowerPoint® presentation (visual and textual)
- ☐ Video presentation (visual)

Requesting the Interview

When you ask someone to do an interview, you must provide some background information on yourself and your project. This will help your interviewee understand your objectives and will make him/her feel comfortable. Answering the questions below will give you the basic information you need to share when you make the request for an interview. Write your answers in the column to the right.

1. What is your name? Where do you live, work, or go to school?	
2. Why are you conducting this interview?	
3. Will you disclose that you are on the autism spectrum? Do you feel it's important to do so? If so, how will you disclose? What will you say?	
4. How did you find out about the person/ advocate you wish to interview?	
5. What will become of your interview? Will you give a report? Will you submit it for publication?	
6. How would you like to conduct the interview? Be prepared to be flexible. Your interviewee might wish to do the interview in a format that isn't your first choice. As the interviewer, it's important to accommodate any special requests, if you can.	

Once you have assembled your information, call or email the person you wish to interview. Remember to provide the person with your contact information, so that he/she can call or email you back. Once you have permission to conduct the interview, you can schedule it at a mutually agreed-upon time and/or place.

Developing Questions for the Interview

Questions for the Profile

For any kind of report, you must include a profile of the person you are interviewing. The profile can be a brief portion of your report, or it can be the main content, depending upon your objective. List at least five questions that you will ask your interviewee in order to gather information for the profile. This can range from what type of work the person does to where he/she lives.

Your Questions	Interviewee's Responses
1.	
2.	
3.	
4.	
5.	

Questions for the Content

Will your interview focus on a particular topic or debate in the autism community? If so, develop at least three questions you wish to ask your interviewee. (If you have trouble developing content questions, you can always use the self-reflection questions that you answered earlier in this unit.)

Your Questions	Interviewee's Responses
1.	
2.	
3.	

 Now you're ready to conduct the interview! Remember to have fun, and good luck! If you like how your report turns out, consider submitting it to the Integrated Self-Advocacy ISA web page for publication (www.valerieparadiz. com/community).

Unit 6

Lesson Title: The Social Scan™

Learning Objectives

- To familiarize students with common social attributes and challenges associated with ASD, with an emphasis on the student perspective
- To teach students how to conduct Social Scans™ at school, at home, at work, or in the community
- To assist students in developing and implementing a Social Advocacy Plan by using the scan data they have collected

Brief Description of Lesson

In "Getting to Know My Social Tendencies," students are introduced to some common social attributes associated with autism spectrum and related conditions. Quite often, social differences present obstacles to participation in class, family life, employment, and community activities. As therapists and educators, we work hard with students to teach "social skills," often through formal curricula or group and individual therapy. However, in doing so, we sometimes leave students out of the loop when it comes to decision-making and advocacy regarding their personal social needs and preferences.

This unit is meant to guide students toward independent social advocacy by introducing them to the concept that our social differences as individuals with autism are not merely a set of deficiencies. Instead, they reflect a *cultural difference* that we must understand in relation to mainstream social expectations. This approach can move students into new arenas of thinking about social options, opening up a larger space for them to advocate for their specific needs in changing environments.

As with the Sensory Scan in Unit 4, students conduct Social Scans using the worksheet provided as a means of understanding their social tendencies in everyday environments.

As an extended lesson, students conduct social scans in additional settings at work, at home, or in the community, and report on the results.

> *With the information gathered from the Social Scan (see **My Social Tendencies** at the bottom of the scan worksheet on pages 47-48 of the Student Workbook), students turn to their individual **Self-Advocacy Portfolios** on page 92 in the Student Workbook to create Advocacy Plans to address their social needs and preferences, such as adjusting the degree of participation in an activity, changing their physical location in relation to others, creating Advocacy Scripts, or identifying and acting on how many people they are able relate to at a given time. The **Self-Advocacy Portfolio** is a living document. Students should continue to repeat Social Scans and write new Advocacy Plans into the portfolio as needed.*

Materials and Other Instructional Needs

- Whiteboard

A. Getting to Know My Social Tendencies

1. Have students take turns reading "Getting to Know My Social Tendencies" aloud from their Student Workbooks.

2. If needed, have students reread the text silently and highlight unknown vocabulary or phrases they wish to discuss.

3. Ask students to write unknown vocabulary words or phrases on the board. Ask for definitions and comments, or supply them as needed and write them on the board for visual support. Students can also copy the vocabulary into their Student Workbooks in the table provided.

4. Next, lead a discussion, offering a preliminary exploration of individual social experiences, needs, and preferences.

Questions you might ask are also listed in the Self-Reflection section of the Student Workbooks.

a. Are you aware of any social tendencies that you have?

b. Is it easy for you to have a conversation with someone one-on-one? How about with a group of two or three? How about a group of four or five? How about a large group? How do you feel in large groups generally?

c. Do you often worry about saying the "wrong" thing? If yes, explain.

d. What kinds of things do you find it difficult to talk about with others?

e. What kinds of things do you enjoy talking about with others?

f. If you could change one thing in this particular setting in terms of how it affects your comfort level socially, what would it be and why?

Getting to Know My Social Tendencies

In the professional literature, individuals diagnosed with autism spectrum conditions are often described as having social deficits or challenges. The people who support us – teachers, therapists, and doctors – are usually aware of our social differences. In fact, many of them are trained to work with us in improving our "social skills." For example, we might participate in a social skills class where we are taught how to make eye contact. Or, we might be asked to monitor and adjust how closely we position our bodies to others when we are in conversation. At other times, we are reminded to say "hello" and "goodbye" when entering or leaving a room, a person, or a group of people.

While these lessons are very important for us to learn, often our therapists and teachers are not trained to be sensitive to our personal social needs and preferences. As individuals on the autism spectrum, it is important that we learn about others' expectations of us socially. Yet, there are times when we must be in tune with our social needs and know how and when to make requests or adjust our social participation so that we may feel more comfortable. Strategies might range from finding a structured activity to engage in so that we can remain in an unstructured social setting, to asking someone to speak with us in a quieter room or a quieter space within the room, to leaving a situation when we feel too overstimulated or socially confused to be happy or comfortable. As we identify and advocate for such preferences or needs, we must be learn to tune into our social tendencies and educate others as we make requests or changes.

Our social settings change continually throughout a day. If you begin to pay attention to the settings you move through, you will learn what your tendencies are; for example, in smaller groups compared to larger groups, with people you know versus strangers, etc. Once you know your tendencies, you'll begin to identify your own particular options. One way to gather this information is to conduct a Social Scan. This is very similar to the Sensory Scan you learned to use in Unit 4.

Taking time to conduct a Social Scan in a new setting, or even in situations in which you find yourself in routinely, such as the classroom or the cafeteria at school, can give you insight into the things that make you feel good socially as well as the things that make you feel anxious or uncomfortable. With such knowledge, you can take steps to feel more at ease throughout the day.

SOCIAL TENDENCIES New Vocabulary and Ideas	
Words or Phrases	**Definitions and Notes**
1.	1.
2.	2.
3.	3.
4.	4.
5.	5.

B. The Social Scan

Using the Social Scan worksheet in their Student Handbooks, students scan a social setting in which they routinely find themselves. Scanning the classroom is a good first step. Remember to provide the option of using electronic worksheets.

The Social Scan™ Worksheet
Integrated Self-Advocacy ISA™

My Personal Information and Scan Location

Your name: _____   Date: _____

School/Grade/Program: _____

Which social environment will you be scanning? _____

The Social Scan

1. **People:** Pay attention to **the people** in this situation. Which of the following apply? Fill in as many details as you can in the Notes sections.

   ☐ How many people are in this environment? If it's a large number, give an estimate.
   Number:

   ☐ There are people I know here. Describe how this makes you feel.
   Notes:

   ☐ I do not know any of the people here. Describe how this makes you feel.
   Notes:

   ☐ Other.
   Notes:

My comfort level with people in this setting is (circle one):			
1	2	3	4
unbearable	uncomfortable	not a problem	comfortable

2. **Structure & Space:** Pay attention to **the structure of this situation and how people are distributed in space in relation to you.** Which of the following apply? Fill in as many details as you can in the Notes sections.

   ☐ This is a formal or organized setting. People are seated in rows of chairs or at table(s) or desk(s).
   Notes:

   ☐ I feel comfortable with the amount of space in relation to the number of people.
   Notes:

   ☐ The setting is not formal or organized. People are moving about at will or standing/sitting in groups.
   Notes:

☐ I feel uncomfortable with the amount of space in relation to the number of people.
Notes:

☐ Provide some details on your location in this setting, as well as your proximity to others.
Notes:

☐ Other
Notes:

My comfort level with the structure of this setting is (circle one):			
1	2	3	4
unbearable	uncomfortable	not a problem	comfortable

3. **Content:** Pay attention to **the content of this social environment**. Which of the following apply? Fill in as many details as you can in the Notes sections.

☐ This is a formal lecture or class, one or more people are speaking to the others, who are listening.
The topic(s) being discussed is/are:

☐ This is an informal setting, such as a party or other loosely organized social gathering.
People are talking about:

☐ This is a very quiet setting. People are either whispering or not talking at all.
Notes:

My comfort level with the content of this setting is (circle one):			
1	2	3	4
unbearable	uncomfortable	not a problem	comfortable

4. **Expectations:** Think about **what might be expected of you** in this environment. Which of the following apply? Fill in as many details as you can in the Notes sections.

☐ I am expected to participate with others in an organized activity.
Notes:

☐ Participation in this situation is voluntary and not expected of me or others.
Notes:

☐ I am not sure what is expected of me.
Notes:

☐ I am expected to be quiet and listen in this setting.
Notes:

☐ Other
Notes:

My comfort level with the expectations this setting is (circle one):			
1	2	3	4
unbearable	uncomfortable	not a problem	comfortable

My Social Tendencies

You will use the results of this questionnaire to create an Advocacy Plan in your *Self-Advocacy Portfolio*.

1. Review your Social Scan. Which social aspects of this setting make you uncomfortable (score of 1 or 2)?

2. Which social aspects of this setting are you comfortable with (score of 3 or 4)?

C. The Social Advocacy Plan

Using the information they have gathered from the Social Scan, students turn to their *Self-Advocacy Portfolios* (page 83 in the Student Workbook) to create a Social Advocacy Plan that includes strategies for addressing social challenges and writing scripts for requesting modifications. The *Self-Advocacy Portfolio* is the backbone of *The Integrated Self-Advocacy ISA Curriculum* and serves as a living document of a student's current advocacy strategies and tools. Students should conduct scans and write advocacy plans as the need arises.

To make students feel more comfortable doing scans, conduct one yourself and report on the results.

D. Extended Lesson: Conduct a Scan at Home or in Your Community

1. Ask students to conduct additional scans using the Social Scan worksheet, at home or in the community, and then bring the results back to school.
2. Lead a group discussion, cueing students to share the data they have gathered.
3. Repeat the steps above for creating a Social Advocacy Plan in the *Self-Advocacy Portfolio*.
4. All copies of Social Scans and Advocacy Plans should be updated periodically and included in the *Self-Advocacy Portfolio*.

Remember, you can offer students the option of using electronic versions of the worksheets and the Self-Advocacy Portfolio *provided on the CD that accompanies this book. Many students with autism spectrum and related conditions can perform better when given the option of working on a computer.*

Unit 7

Lesson Title: Identifying and Cultivating Strengths and Focused Interests

Learning Objectives

- To identify, validate, and encourage students' strengths and focused interests
- To provide a forum for exploring how interests can be helpful tools in self-regulation
- To explore vocational directions involving focused interests

Brief Description of Lesson

In this unit, students are provided with a forum for sharing and exploring their strengths, passions, and focused interests. Many individuals with ASD enjoy engaging in activities or areas of knowledge with great attention or repetitiveness. As educators, we might judge these interests too quickly as nonfunctional, obsessive, or as having little significance in practical life, such as video gaming, memorizing facts, or engaging in media fixations. However, these interests sometimes hold hidden potential for individuals on the spectrum – as tools for self-regulation, as a means of understanding and navigating the social landscape, or as precursors for vocational directions they might wish to pursue.

After working through a guided reading on identifying and exploring their strengths and focused interests, students conduct a research project involving vocational possibilities. As an expanded lesson, students visit a workplace in their community where they interview someone who works in a field that has commonalities with their interests.

Materials and Other Instructional Needs

- Whiteboard
- Video camera
- Audio recording device
- AV setup for viewing videos or listening to audio interviews
- Internet access

A. *Identifying and Cultivating Strengths and Focused Interests*

1. Have students begin this unit by working through the guided reading and activities found in "Identifying Strengths and Focused Interests." Provide support when necessary.

2. If needed, have students read the text more than once, highlighting unknown vocabulary or phrases they wish to discuss.

3. Ask students to write unknown vocabulary words or phrases they wish to discuss on the board. Ask for definitions and comments, or supply them as needed and write them on the board for visual support. Students can also copy the vocabulary into their Student Workbooks in the table provided.

4. Lead a discussion, supporting students in an exploration of individual passions, strengths, and focused interests – past and present. *By the end of the discussion, make sure each student has chosen one current interest to focus on for the final segments of the unit.*

5. Ask students to continue with the second guided reading, "Focused Interests Can Be Useful." Students should work independently through this segment, with support as needed. Repeat the steps involving new vocabulary and questions as outlined in #2-3.

6. Ask students to read "Focused Interests and Careers." If necessary, repeat steps #2-3.

7. Finally, ask students to complete the Focused Interests and Careers worksheet. Follow this with a discussion, asking students to share the results of their research.

8. Ask students to transfer the career they feel suits them best to the Transition Planning section of the *Self-Advocacy Portfolio* on page 96 in the Student Workbook.

You might find that some students have trouble choosing one career to research. This is because they may think you are asking them to be certain. If this happens, it can be helpful to offer insight into vocational development and the fact that it is a process. The Self-Advocacy Portfolio is designed to absorb changes and reflect this process. At any time, students can (and should!) change and update the information they have in the portfolio.

Identifying and Cultivating Strengths and Focused Interests

Are there activities that you like to do a lot? Are there areas of knowledge that you would be happy to read, think, or talk about most of the day (if you could)? Perhaps you have several interests that are important to you just about every day of your life.

As someone on the autism spectrum, your chances of having thought processes and needs involving repeated viewings of videos or frequent engagement with specific topics, television programs, music, or electronic games are high. In fact, such passions and focused interests are common to many on the spectrum. We don't all have the same interests, but there are some identifiable trends among us. On the following page are a few of those trends. If you see your interests (past or present) listed, make a few notes about them in the Notes section of the table provided. If you don't see your interests, add your own in the space provided.

Next, choose the most favorite interest that you are **currently** pursuing. If you don't have a favorite, select one interest that you would like to focus on as the main theme for the remainder of this unit and write it here:

My Strength or Focused Interest: _____

Area of Interest	Notes
Music	
Video Gaming	
Fantasy	
Television Programs	
Films	
Comedy	
Animation	
Comic Books and/or Animé	
Mechanics/Engineering	
Math	
Science	
Computer Software, IT, or Programming	
Animals	
Foreign Languages	
Reading and Literature	

B. *Focused Interests Can Be Useful*

Focused Interests Can Be Useful

In the literature about autism, our focused interests are sometimes referred to as obsessions or perseveration. One dictionary definition of the word "perseveration" is: "a tendency to repeat the response to an experience in later situations where it is not appropriate." It is true that at times we think about or engage in a focused interest in situations where others don't understand its significance. It might seem out of context to them, and they might even judge us negatively or think we are weird.

However, many individuals with autism have reported that they often turn to their focused interests or areas of strength for very important reasons. For example, sometimes our interests can provide structure in social situations that are new, challenging, or confusing. We might find it helpful in such settings to talk with others about an area of interest we know well, especially if we are not sure what we are "supposed" to do or say. It might help us feel less anxious. Additionally, some aspies and auties report that they generally feel most comfortable talking about facts and content rather than about personal information, feelings, or "chit chat." Therefore, turning to our interests in conversation might provide us with the content we need to feel comfortable in such situations.

Many individuals with autism also feel that their focused interests can be useful for self-regulation. You might be thinking: "Self-regulation? What the heck is that?" Well, some of us become overly stimulated when sensory or social environments become difficult for us to navigate or are stressful. In fact, the sensory and social scans we did in previous units were tools for self-regulation. Once you identified elements in a given environment that could be adjusted or addressed in some fashion, you were able to feel more relaxed in that setting. In other words, you **self-regulated**. Someone didn't do it for you; you did it independently. This is the heart and soul of becoming a self-advocate!

Sometimes aspies and auties turn to their focused interests or passions to decompress after a long day at school or work. Many of us play video games; others like to engage in an area of knowledge they are deeply interested in, such as reading up on the history of the railroads, reading fantasy novels, or memorizing jokes from joke books. Sometimes we like to repeat segments of scripts we have heard in films as a means of feeling more centered in our bodies and thoughts.

Can you think of times when you might do this yourself? How frequently do you engage in your interests? Where do you engage in your interests? These are important questions to ask because they help us become more self-aware.

Our deep interests can be useful to us, but they can be confusing to others around us. We need to watch out for signs of misunderstanding as best we can, in order to make decisions about how and where we might wish to pursue our interests and whether they can be integrated into a setting without being a disruption to others – while remaining the helpful support they are to us. Other times, it's simply safe to not engage in a focused interest in specific settings. Can you think of reasons why?

Another important word of caution about focused interests is that we must be careful to look for signs of depression in ourselves, which might lead to wanting to engage in our interests for very long periods of time while other important opportunities or aspects of life pass us by. If you have been feeling sad and alone, your interest might be a support to you, but it also might be keeping you from getting the help you need to address your isolation. Most things in life have their downsides as well as their upsides. This is true of focused interests. That's why it's important to recognize how your interests play a role in your day-to-day routines at work, in school, and in your relationships with loved ones, friends, colleagues, and even people you've just met for the first time.

FOCUSED INTERESTS New Vocabulary and Ideas	
Words or Phrases	**Definitions and Notes**
1.	1.
2.	2.
3.	3.
4.	4.
5.	5.

C. Researching a Focused Interest

Focused Interests and Careers

Now that you have identified your interests and have chosen one to explore more deeply, let's conduct an investigation into how that interest could be a precursor to a job or other career direction for you. Temple Grandin, an individual with autism, used to have focused interests in mechanical things, such as automatic, sliding glass doors. When she was a little girl, she liked watching automatic doors move open and closed repeatedly. Later in life, Temple became one of the most sought-after engineers in the animal processing and facility design industry. Her clients are big corporations like McDonald's. In addition to engineering, she has focused interests in livestock and in the places where these animals are raised and prepared for butchering. She is particularly interested in making the process of butchering more humane, so that animals do not experience intense fear and anxiety before they die. In her memoir, *Thinking in Pictures*, Temple writes about how her early passion for mechanical things, like the sliding glass doors, was a precursor to the work she does today. And in her book *Developing Talents – Careers for Individuals with Asperger Syndrome and High-Functioning Autism,* she gives numerous other examples of how individuals on the spectrum have used their special interests to build careers.

Your own interests might be precursors to a future career in the same way they were for Temple. Therefore, it's worth exploring them to find out. You can do this by filling in the following Focused Interests and Careers worksheet.

D. Extended Lesson

Assist your students in identifying someone in your community who works in a field related to their top career choice. Help make plans for students to visit these persons on the job. Alternatively, students can request to interview the person, using the Interview worksheet from Unit 5. Ask students to offer a summary report of the visit in writing or other media (PowerPoint®, video or audio interview, etc.).

Focused Interests and Careers
Integrated Self-Advocacy ISA™

My Strength or Focused Interest

Your name: _____ Date: _____

Your interest: _____

	Career #1	Career #2	Career #3
STEP 1: DIRECTIONS List 3 possible career directions that relate to your chosen interest.			
STEP 2: EDUCATION & TRAINING Using the Internet or a library, find out the level of education you need for this job, including special certificates or training.			
STEP 3: SKILLS & CONSIDERATIONS Which additional skills must you have to do well at this job? People skills? Ability to work collaboratively? Ability to work independently? Ability to tolerate stressful environments? Ability to work in challenging sensory environments? Skill in creating social networks with co-workers?			

My Top Career Choice

    STEP 4: TOP CAREER CHOICE

Review the information you gathered above. Using this information, choose the career direction you feel you'd be most capable of, and interested in, pursuing. Keep your sensory and social needs in mind as you make your choice! Transfer this career choice to the Transition Planning section of your *Self-Advocacy Portfolio* on page 96.

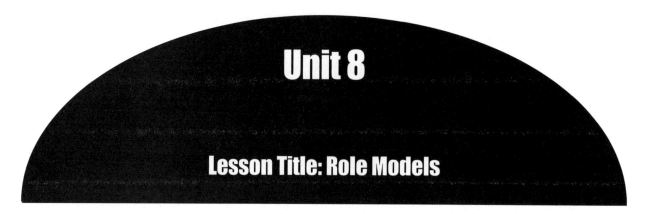

Unit 8

Lesson Title: Role Models

Learning Objectives

- To familiarize students with historical figures who, if they were alive today, might be diagnosed with an autism spectrum disorder
- To explore the concept of "cultural autism"
- To acknowledge and celebrate our contributions as individuals with ASD to the autism community, as well as to mainstream culture

Brief Description of Lesson

In the essay, "What Is a Role Model?" students read about the concept of role models and explore why people turn to role models for inspiration and guidance. After choosing a role model who is important to them, students conduct research on that figure (historical or contemporary), and create a PowerPoint® presentation to share with the group. The extended lesson includes a choice of reading assignments from books that profile historical figures who had autism or possessed characteristics of autism.

Materials and Other Instructional Needs

- Whiteboard
- Internet access
- PowerPoint® software application

A. What Is a Role Model?

In Unit 5 we studied the history of autism from a social and medical perspective. In this unit, history also plays a role, but the focus is on individuals, their biographies, and their achievements as people on the spectrum.

1. Have students take turns reading aloud from "What Is a Role Model?" in their Student Workbooks.

2. If needed, ask students to reread the text silently and highlight unknown vocabulary and words or phrases they wish to discuss.

3. Ask students to write unknown vocabulary words on the board. Ask for definitions or supply them as needed and write them on the board for visual support. Students can also copy the vocabulary into their Student Workbooks in the table provided.

4. Lead a discussion, reinforcing the self-advocacy goals of this lesson.

    Questions you might ask are also listed in the Self-Reflection section of the Student Workbooks.

   a. What is a role model?
   b. Do you have a role model?
   c. Why is this person a model to you?

5. By the end of the discussion, be sure that each student has chosen a role model for the research project outlined in segment B of the unit. Students do not have to choose individuals diagnosed with or thought to have autism.

What Is a Role Model?

If you had to explain what a role model is in your own words, what would you say? Do you have a role model? What attracted you to this person's life? Sociologists define role models as people we compare ourselves to because we aspire to be like them or because their actions and behavior are things we value and want to emulate. Social movements of almost any kind (the women's movement, the disability movement, or the gay and lesbian movement, for example) look to role models as a means of maintaining strength and purpose in their efforts to effect change or raise awareness. For African Americans, Dr. Martin Luther King is perhaps one of the most significant role models. For people with disabilities, former president Franklin Delano Roosevelt can be an inspiration, and in the gay and lesbian community, Harvey Milk, former councilman of San Francisco, might come to mind. Both Martin Luther King and Harvey Milk were assassinated for their beliefs and for being such powerful instruments of change in society, but becoming a martyr for a cause is not a requirement for becoming a role model to others! On the other hand, many important figures in history who inspire us are often individuals who took great risks in order to achieve a goal or accomplish something that enriched many lives. Some role models might inspire us not only due to their moral behavior but also because of their accomplishments, such inventors or artists. As you can see, the concept of the role model is quite broad. Your neighbor, your dad, or your aunt could be a role model to you.

Individuals with ASD often look to Temple Grandin as a role model for the very reasons mentioned above. Temple was one of the first autistic people to publicly share her experiences and educate others about our challenges and strengths. This took a great deal of courage. Her accomplishments in the fields of engineering and animal science inspire other individuals on the spectrum and their families, not to mention neurotypcial professionals who work in her field.

In the book *Genius Genes: How Asperger Talents Changed the World*, authors Michael Fitzgerald and Brendan O'Brien profile various historical figures who made significant contributions to advancing the arts and sciences. What makes Fitzgerald's and O'Brien's book so interesting is that it shows how people like Charles Darwin, Thomas Jefferson, and Isaac Newton had characteristics associated with autism and how these very traits actually played a role in the contributions they made.

In *Elijah's Cup*, writer Valerie Paradiz (that's me, the author of this book!) invites us to look at the lives of the visual artist Andy Warhol, the physicist Albert Einstein, the comedian Andy Kaufman, and the philosopher Ludwig Wittgenstein through "autistic lenses." Were they living today, these men might be considered to be individuals on the spectrum.

Andy Warhol, for example, had strongly focused interests in art and sketching from a very young age. As a boy, he would spend many hours in his bedroom after school making drawings. He was also considered to be socially "eccentric," both in childhood and in his adult years, by peers and colleagues, and he had such a keen sense of smell that he could identify the type of perfumes women wore as they whisked past him on the streets of New York (sensory acuity). Like Warhol, Albert Einstein had deep interests, specifically in music and physics. He also seems to have had learning differences because he received terrible grades in school, except for physics and music, in which he excelled. He wasn't allowed to study at college in Germany (where he was born) because of his poor grades; however, he did get accepted into a Swiss technical institute. Later he developed the famous theory of relativity while living in Switzerland and working in a patent office, often wearing his slippers to work (probably due to sensory needs).

In the next segment of this unit, you will conduct research on a role model who is important to you. It doesn't have to be someone on the spectrum, but if you'd like to do research on a person who has autism, or might have been autistic, you can ask your teacher for suggestions. Write the name of your role model below.

My Role Model: _____

ROLE MODEL New Vocabulary and Ideas	
Words or Phrases	**Definitions and Notes**
1.	1.
2.	2.
3.	3.
4.	4.
5.	5.

D. Research Project and PowerPoint® Presentation

1. Students conduct research using the Internet, following the Role Model worksheet provided in their Student Workbooks.
2. Students create PowerPoint® presentations, using the information they have gathered.
3. Students present PowerPoint® presentations to the class.

 Remember, you can offer students the option of using electronic versions of the worksheets and the Self-Advocacy Portfolio provided on the CD that accompanies this book. Many students with autism spectrum and related conditions can perform better when given the option of working on a computer.

Role Model Worksheet
Integrated Self-Advocacy ISA™

My Personal Information & Role Model

Your name: _____   Today's date: _____

Your role model: _____

Biographical Information
Using the Internet or a library, conduct research on your role model's biography and answer the questions below.

1. Date of birth and death:

2. Country and city born in:

3. Other locations that this person lived or was active in work or other endeavors:

4. What was this person's childhood like? List at least 3 facts.

    •

    •

    •

5. What was this person's adult life like? List at least 3 facts.

    •

    •

    •

Inspiration
List three reasons why you chose this person to research as a role model. Offer information on the person's accomplishments, moral character, or other things he/she has done, written, or said that inspire you. If you find images or quotations on the Web that might be helpful as elements for PowerPoint® presentation, save or record them.

1.

2.

3.

Presentation
Create a PowerPoint® presentation by translating each of your answers above into individual slides. Your presentation should include a title slide, plus eight additional slides to cover your answers. In some of the slides use images or quotations that you saved from the Internet. Present the facts you gathered as bullet points, so that when you do your presentation, you can refer to them.

Instead of creating PowerPoint® presentations, students may wish to write an essay, or report orally to the class on their findings, using the Role Model worksheet as a guide.

C. Extended Lesson: Suggested Readings

Students can choose to read selected chapters from books that profile historical figures who might have been on the autism spectrum. Below is a list of resources. Additionally, students can use the Role Model Worksheet to collect information and then report on the individual(s) they have read about.

Encourage students to submit articles or essays about their role models to the editors of the Integrated Self-Advocacy ISA web site (www.valerieparadiz. com/community) to be considered for publication. A good résumé builder!

Fitzgerald, M., & O'Brien, B. (2007). *Genius genes: How Asperger talents changed the world.* Shawnee Mission, KS: Autism Asperger Publishing Company.

Grandin, T. (1995). *Thinking in pictures and other reports from my life with autism.* New York: Doubleday.

Grandin, T., & Duffy, K. (2008). *Developing talents – Careers for individuals with Asperger Syndrome and high-functioning autism.* Shawnee Mission, KS: Autism Asperger Publishing Company.

Paradiz, V. (2005). *Elijah's cup: A family's journey into the community and culture of high functioning autism and Asperger's Syndrome.* London: Jessica Kingsley Publishers.

Ledgin, N. (2000). *Diagnosing Jefferson.* Arlington, TX: Future Horizons.

Ledgin, N. (2002). *Asperger's and self-esteem: Insight and hope through famous role models.* Arlington, TX: Future Horizons.

Unit 9

Lesson Title: Autism in the Media

Learning Objectives

- To familiarize students with basic skills in media literacy, including critical analysis
- To review and reinforce the concept of "perspective," including an exploration of attribution and how individuals with ASD process different media messages
- To explore and validate student views on media reporting about autism

Brief Description of Lesson

After completing a guided introduction to the basic elements of media literacy and analysis, students view, read, or listen to three reports involving the topic of autism. Students analyze each report using the Media Analysis worksheet, followed by group discussion. In the extended lesson, students translate one media analysis, including their personal commentary, into written, video, or audio commentary.

Materials and Other Instructional Needs

- AV equipment for viewing or listening to audio or visual media
- Internet access
- Whiteboard

A. Introduction to Media Literacy

1. Lead a discussion by first asking students, "What is the 'media'?" Ask them to offer examples of different types of media. Write the examples on the whiteboard as shown in the diagram called "Types of Media" below and cue students to write them in their Student Workbooks in the space provided. Some examples are provided below.

2. Some media types fit into more than one category. Encourage students to first list the primary type, then secondary type(s).

3. Ask students to read "Autism in the Media" in their Student Workbooks. If needed, students can reread the text silently and highlight unknown vocabulary and words or phrases they wish to discuss.

4. Ask students to complete, with your assistance, the diagram called "Concepts in Media Literacy." Cue students to provide definitions of words or explanations of ideas and supply them as needed on the board for visual support.

TYPES OF MEDIA	
Type of Media	**Category: Print, Audio, or Visual**
Newspaper	Print (sometimes visual: photos)
Radio	Audio
Podcast	Audio
YouTube	Visual
Television (News or Programs)	Visual
Television Commercials or Public Service Announcements	Visual
Magazine	Print (sometimes visual: photos)
Blog	Print (sometimes visual: photos)
Film	Visual

Autism in the Media

Now that you have an understanding of the wide variety of media that we are exposed to in our daily lives, take a moment to think about whether you have ever read an article or seen a report that involved the topic of autism. Perhaps you've watched an episode from a television program that featured a character with autism, or maybe you saw a news-hour feature on a medical issue, like vaccines or the high incidence of autism diagnoses. How did you feel when you saw or read the program or report? Did you feel it fairly represented your experience? Or was the perspective presented more focused on a parent's story or a professional's view of autism?

If you've never seen, read, or heard media that involves autism or Asperger Syndrome, you will have an opportunity to do so in this unit. In fact, you will also have an opportunity to analyze different types of media to understand whether a story has a particular bias, who the audience is meant to be, and whether or not it represents, in your opinion, a fair and accurate representation of what it's like to be autistic. All of these activities involve developing "media literacy," or your ability to view, read or listen to media critically.

"Why is this so important?" you might wonder. To begin with, autism has been a very "hot topic" in the media in the past several years, and since all the reporting and programming has to do with you, it is a good idea to get an understanding of how mainstream culture is presented with representations of who you are, what you're like, and how others imagine those of us on the spectrum to be.

The majority of reports and programs that deal with autism are not produced or written by individuals with autism. This is a significant fact that all of us on the spectrum must take into account. We might agree or disagree with what others make us out to be, or how they portray our relationships with our parents or others. Developing an opinion is important. Doing so will not only help you navigate the media with tools, but it will also validate your own views. After all, you're the person on the spectrum, right? Finally, developing a critical approach to the media might give you some ideas for producing or writing your own projects involving the topic of autism.

CONCEPTS IN MEDIA LITERACY	
Point of View	
Bias	
Intended Audience	
Representation	
Message or Intention	

B. Analyzing the Media

1. Screen a short media clip that reports on a topic involving autism. YouTube and other Web-based outlets can be good sources for clips.

2. Screen the clip again, this time asking students to complete a Media Analysis worksheet in their Student Workbooks.

3. Follow up the analysis with a discussion.

4. Screen additional clips or provide other sources of media, such as print or radio stories. Ask students to complete additional Media Analysis worksheets for each article, report or story.

5. With the completion of each screening or other media review, cue students to share the results of their analyses in group discussions. Encourage comparative analysis of two or more worksheet results.

Questions you might ask are also listed in the Self-Reflection section of Student Workbooks.

a. Do you agree or disagree with the point of view presented in this media example? Why?

b. How do you feel about the language or images used to describe individuals with autism?

c. If you could ask the person who produced or wrote this media one question, what would it be?

 For students with processing challenges, play or screen audio and visual clips as many times as needed.

If necessary, reduce the number of media analyses that students must conduct, or take more than one class period to cover more media sources. An important point in this exercise is to offer students sources to compare, so that they begin to see the variety of perspectives on autism in the media.

Media Analysis Worksheet
Integrated Self-Advocacy ISA™

Your Information & Media Description

Your name: _____   Date: _____

Title of program or story:_____

Type of media: _____   Date of media:_____

Media Analysis

Who is the author, director, and/or producer?	
What is the name of the program, magazine, or newspaper where this media appeared?	
What is the estimated circulation or number of viewers? If you don't know, indicate whether this is prime time television program, a mainstream newspaper, etc.	
Who is the intended audience?	
What is the point of view? (parent, professional, person with autism)	
What is the message of the media, or its intended purpose?	
Is an individual with autism depicted in this media? If so, how?	
What kind of language or images are used to describe autism or individuals with autism?	
Do you feel this media represents autism and/or individuals with autism accurately? Why or why not?	
Do you feel this media represents autism and/or individuals with autism fairly? Why or why not?	
How did this media story or article make you feel?	
Other pertinent information or comments you wish to add.	

C. Extended Lesson

1. Ask students to choose one of the media analyses they have completed. Using this information, students create a commentary on the media they viewed, read, or listened to. The commentary can be presented as an article, or as an audio or video opinion piece.

2. Commentaries may be submitted to the editors of the Integrated Self-Advocacy ISA web site at www.valerieparadiz.com/community for possible publication – a great résumé builder!

Unit 10

Lesson Title: Becoming a Part of Your IEP

Learning Objectives

- To understand the basics of the Individuals with Disabilities Education Act (IDEA) and the purpose of the Individualized Education Program (IEP)
- To explore options and make plans for attending or otherwise representing oneself at an IEP meeting

Brief Description of Lesson

In schools, students with disabilities are encouraged to attend their annual IEP meetings, yet as educators we often do not provide them with the information or support they need to participate in a meaningful way. The purpose of this lesson is to inspire and motivate students to become an integral part of their IEP development. As you teach this unit, think of yourself as a role model for that inspiration.

After reading "Becoming a Part of Your IEP," students explore options and plan for how they will participate in their next IEP meeting by completing two guided worksheets. The expanded lesson includes a word search puzzle that reinforces key concepts learned in this unit.

Materials and Other Instructional Needs

- Whiteboard
- Computers

A. Becoming a Part of Your IEP

 Important Note: In group settings, a 1:1 session with a teacher or therapist to review individual and confidential aspects of the IEP is recommended before proceeding with the lesson.

1. Have students take turns reading "Becoming a Part of Your Own IEP" aloud.

2. Ask students to fill out the Exploring Options worksheet in their Student Workbooks. This worksheet walks students through the various options they have for attending their own IEP meeting or having someone represent them, if they do not wish to attend.

    When students have completed this worksheet, they should transfer the information contained in the box at the bottom of the worksheet to page 94 of the *Self-Advocacy Portfolio* in the Student Workbook.

3. Ask students to answer questions about themselves and their current school placement using the IEP Statement worksheet provided in their Student Workbooks. Students should answer the questions in full sentences. (This will make preparing the IEP statement easier.)

4. Before the IEP meeting, have students adapt their IEP statement into a document that can be submitted and/or read aloud at the IEP meeting. In most cases, students can simply transcribe the answers to the questions, stringing them together in a single essay.

    When students have completed this worksheet, they should copy their personal statements to page 94 of the *Self-Advocacy Portfolio* in the Student Workbook.

5. Ask a teacher or therapist who is attending the IEP meeting to support the student in explaining his or her needs and preferences, based on the outcome of the Exploring Options worksheet. Allow students to choose whether they would like a staff person to speak on their behalf or whether they would like to do so themselves.

6. After the IEP meeting, you might wish to follow up with some questions. The questions below are also included in the Self-Reflection section of the Student Workbooks.

   a. Do you feel more informed about your IEP and your school? If yes, what have you learned that's new?
   b. Will you attend your IEP meeting next year? If so, would you change the way you want to participate?
   c. If you asked a representative to attend your meeting and share your personal statement, did your representative give you any feedback on how the meeting went? If not, ask the person who represented you to summarize so that you have an idea of the results of your good efforts!

Becoming a Part of Your IEP

Do you know what an IEP is? You have probably heard this acronym at some point in your career as a student, but did you know that the IEP is probably one of the most important things that affects your life in school? If this comes as a surprise to you, that's O.K. If it doesn't, that's O.K., too. Our purpose is to be sure that every student who has an IEP knows about this important document. Are you curious?

IEP stands for Individualized Education Program. "Huh? What's that?" Well, because you are diagnosed with an autism spectrum condition, your school is required by the federal government to provide you with an Individualized Education Program. The legislation that created this mandate happened way back in 1975, when Congress passed the Individuals with Disabilities Education Act (IDEA). This is the law that says kids with disabilities have the right to attend public schools and receive specific, individual support from their teachers and therapists. The details are all outlined in your IEP. If you want to see your IEP and learn more about it, you can ask an adult in your life to sit down and explain it to you. It can be your mom or dad or a grandparent, or it can be one of the teachers or therapists in your school.

Your IEP is updated every year, and at least once each year a meeting is held to review your IEP and to check on how it's going for you in school. Some of the things you find in an IEP are the kind of school you attend (private, public) and the kind of classroom you are in (self-contained, general ed., special ed.). For example, your IEP might list how many teachers and teaching assistants are in your classroom at any given time, or it might indicate whether you are included in classes that aren't only for special ed. students. This is sometimes called "inclusion" or "integration." The IEP also lists the related services you receive in school, such as regularly scheduled meetings with a speech pathologist or an occupational therapist, or if you attend a social skills group a specific number of times each week. Your IEP can also specify important things like allowing extended time when you take exams or do homework.

Changes and updates are made to your IEP in a yearly meeting. Sometimes your parents – or other people who care about you and your comfort and education in school – attend these meetings to offer their input. Did you know that *you* may attend your own IEP meeting? This is a piece of information that the adults in our lives sometimes forget to tell us about. If it sounds like a boring prospect to you, think about it again. Ask yourself: "Are there things about my school, my classes, my social life, and my free time that I really like and would not want to change? Are there things I don't like? Are these things I would like to request be changed?" At an IEP meeting, you can express your views on all of these things.

The activities in this unit can help you decide how you want to participate in your IEP meeting and what you should share with others attending the meeting.

Exploring IEP Options
Integrated Self-Advocacy ISA™

Personal Information

Your name: _____   Today's date: _____

Date of your IEP meeting: _____

Exploring Options Checklist

A. You should feel comfortable and supported when it comes to participating in your IEP meeting. This checklist will help you think about your needs and preferences. Be true to yourself as you consider the scenarios below. Make check marks in all the boxes that apply to you. If you check more than one box, that's O.K. You can decide which of the options is your top choice later.	
Scenario: Make a Check ✔	
1. I can sit comfortably at a conference table with as many as 4-10 people. Most of them are my teachers, my parents, or school administrators. Most of the participants will talk and share opinions. I can sit for the entire time. (This could range from 30 minutes to 2 hours.)	
2. I can sit comfortably at a conference table with as many as 4-10 people. Most of them are my teachers, my parents, or school administrators. Most of the participants will talk and share opinions. Occasionally, I will want to stand up and walk around the room a little, and then return to my chair.	
3. I prefer to stand near the conference table while others are talking and sharing their opinions. Occasionally, I will walk around the room a little.	
4. I prefer to be in the room, with an opportunity to pace. This helps me focus and feel comfortable.	
5. I prefer to stand at the threshold of the doorway while others are talking and sharing their opinions. Occasionally, I will step outside the door for a brief break, then return to the meeting.	
6. I have other or additional needs for attending the meeting than those listed above. I prefer to attend the meeting as follows (add your information here):	
7. I do not wish to attend the meeting, but would like a representative to read a statement on my behalf.	
8. I do not wish to attend the meeting, but would like to prepare an audio recording to be played by a representative on my behalf.	
9. I do not wish to attend the meeting, but would like to prepare a video recording to be screened by a representative on my behalf.	
10. I do not wish to attend the meeting, but would like to participate as follows (fill in your information here):	

B. If you have decided to physically attend your IEP meeting, make check marks in all the boxes that apply to you below. If you check more than one box, that's O.K. You can decide which of the scenarios is your top choice later. (If you aren't attending your meeting in person, skip this section and move on to the box at the bottom of this page.)

Scenario: Make a Check ✔	
1. I would like someone to join me at the meeting for moral support. This person is:	
2. I would like someone to join me at the meeting for support in communication. This person is:	
3. I would like someone to assist me in communicating my personal statement at the meeting. This person is:	
4. I would like to attend my IEP meeting on my own, without a support person.	

5. When I attend my meeting, I will:	a. ☐ Read my personal statement aloud b. ☐ Distribute copies of my personal statement c. ☐ Have my support person assist me in communicating d. ☐ Be present and listen, but not talk e. ☐ Other:
6. When I attend my IEP meeting, I will:	a. ☐ Participate for the entire meeting (This could be 30 minutes to 2 hours, depending upon the number of items that will be discussed.) b. ☐ Stay only for the beginning of the meeting. How many minutes? _____ c. ☐ Have the option to leave any time I choose, so that I can remain comfortable and happy.

My IEP Meeting Plan

Review your answers to parts A and B above. Summarize the details of your plan for being a part of your IEP meeting below. Transfer this information to the IEP section of your *Self-Advocacy Portfolio*.

A:

B:

Next, answer the questions in the following worksheet, using full sentences. If it's easier to use a computer or other keyboard device, ask your teacher to provide one. When you complete these steps, presto! You'll have a personal statement that you can use for your IEP meeting!

IEP Statement Worksheet
Integrated Self-Advocacy ISA™

Your Information

Your name: _____   Today's date: _____

Date of your IEP meeting:_____

Gathering Information for the IEP Statement

Answer the following questions using *full sentences*. If it's easier to use a computer or other keyboard device, ask your teacher to provide one. When you complete these steps, presto! You'll have a personal statement that you can use for your IEP meeting.	
What is your name?	
What grade are you in?	
How long have you been attending the school you go to?	
What is one of your favorite hobbies or deep interests? Give an example of how you engage in your interest.	
How many students are in your classroom? If you go to various classrooms throughout the day, does the number of students in each class vary? What is the number of students you feel most comfortable with in a classroom in order to be able to participate and to feel comfortable?	
Are there some classrooms you like better than others? Why?	
Are there some classrooms or other rooms in the school building that are challenging due to the environment? If so, can changes be made to the environment to increase your comfort there?	
How do you feel about the cafeteria? Do you go there for lunch? What is it like? Would you want to change this?	
Do you feel you get enough breaks in the day to be able to focus in class? If yes, simply state this. If no, offer a suggestion on what you'd like changed in terms of breaks during the day.	
Do you ride the bus to school each day? Is it a crowded bus, or a smaller bus with only a few students? Do you feel comfortable in the bus? If no, explain what makes you uncomfortable.	

What is it like for you in the hallways in your school? Is it loud, confusing, or do you feel comfortable in the hallways?	
Has another student bullied you or called you bad names, like "retard" or some other derogatory word? How did it make you feel? What do you think the school can do to make it better for you in the hallways?	
Do you have friends at your school? What kinds of things do you like to do with them? Do you ever see them after school or on the weekends? If you don't have friends, would you like the school to work on supporting you in making friendships or joining clubs and other activities?	
Do you like the school you go to? Do you want to continue going to your current school? If yes, why? If no, why?	

Identifying Top Requests

Reread all of your answers to the questions above. Based on this information, try to write at least three simple requests or changes that you would like your teachers and the school administrators to consider. You can begin a request with a choice of phrases, such as those listed here (or you can make up your own):

    a.   "I would feel more comfortable if ..."
    b.   "I would be able to participate more in class if ..."
    c.   "I would be more a part of my school if ..."

1.   I would ...

2.   I would ...

3.   I would ...

Compile Your IEP Meeting Statement

You are nearly finished!

Next, take all your answers from above and string them together into one long essay on a separate piece of paper (or on the computer or other keyboard device). Remember to add your three requests at the end of the text. Your personal statement is born! Be sure to keep a copy of this statement in the IEP section of your *Self-Advocacy Portfolio* on page 94.

C. Extended Lesson: Word Search

Find the words or acronyms in the list below in vertical, horizontal, or diagonal directions.

Word List

IEP	IDEA	OT	SLP
integration	self contained	inclusion	related services
social skills	extended time	private	public

r	e	l	a	t	e	d	s	e	r	v	i	c	e	s
f	x	r	w	x	v	l	o	o	o	n	n	e	m	e
m	t	l	s	k	j	h	c	v	z	q	c	x	p	l
x	e	c	l	v	b	n	i	m	q	w	l	e	r	f
o	n	i	p	r	i	v	a	t	e	u	u	y	t	c
p	d	a	s	d	f	g	l	h	j	k	s	l	m	o
g	e	f	d	s	a	z	s	x	c	v	i	b	n	n
h	d	j	k	l	p	i	k	o	u	y	o	t	t	t
x	t	z	p	u	b	l	i	c	q	w	n	e	r	a
c	i	d	e	a	v	b	l	n	m	q	w	e	r	i
f	m	g	h	j	k	l	l	p	o	i	u	y	t	n
b	e	q	b	q	x	r	s	u	i	x	l	g	m	e
i	n	t	e	g	r	a	t	i	o	n	w	t	j	d

Answer Key:

Unit 11

Lesson Title: Understanding How ADA Works in Your Life

Learning Objectives

- To introduce students to the Americans with Disabilities Act (ADA)
- To inform students of their rights regarding employment, access, accommodation, and public services
- To help students understand that the ADA does not automatically ensure that they will be treated equitably as individuals with disabilities, but that they must be active participants in preserving their own civil rights

Brief Description of Lesson

In Unit 10, we learned about students' educational rights under IDEA, which included an introduction to the IEP. This unit prepares students for life after school, when the Americans with Disabilities Act (ADA) becomes the single most important piece of legislation regarding their civil rights. In the essay "Understanding the Americans with Disabilities Act," students learn about the basic components of the ADA. To reinforce key concepts, students complete a brief self-test. For the expanded lesson, students can learn more about the ADA by completing a crossword puzzle that incorporates new vocabulary and ideas.

Materials and Other Instructional Needs

- Whiteboard

A. Understanding the Americans with Disabilities Act

1. Have students take turns reading aloud from "Understanding the Americans with Disabilities Act" in their Student Workbooks.

2. If needed, have students reread the text silently and highlight unknown vocabulary and words or phrases they wish to discuss.

3. Ask students to write unknown vocabulary words on the board. Ask for definitions or supply them as needed. Write them on the board for visual support. Students can also copy the vocabulary into their Student Workbooks in the table provided.

4. Lead a discussion, reinforcing the self-advocacy goals of this lesson.

    Questions you might ask are also listed in the Self-Reflection section of Student Workbooks.

   a. Have you, or has anyone you know, experienced a form of discrimination? Share the story.
   b. If you were applying for a job, would you disclose your disability right away, would you wait until after you were employed, or would you never disclose? Would your decision depend on the situation? Explain your thoughts on this.
   c. Name one thing that you feel would be a good point to teach others in an awareness campaign that aimed at ensuring the civil rights of individuals with autism.

5. Ask students to complete the self-test as a means of reinforcing key concepts. Students may work independently or in pairs. After students have completed the test, share the correct answers in a class discussion.

Understanding the Americans with Disabilities Act

The Americans with Disabilities Act (ADA) is the most comprehensive piece of legislation that protects of the civil rights of individuals with disabilities. It was enacted and signed into law on July 26, 1990. If you think about it, that wasn't very long ago. This is an important point to keep in mind, particularly because social reform, regardless of whether it is mandated by law, doesn't happen overnight. Even with the ADA enacted, individuals on the autism spectrum experience discrimination every day – in school, at college or university, in public settings, and at work. Sometimes the discrimination is intentional, but most of the time it happens because the culture at large is uniformed about autism. The average person does not know how to relate to an individual on the spectrum, let alone what accommodations and mandates are stipulated by the ADA. However, some people and entities, such as employers, public institutions, or universities, are bound by law to know their responsibilities regarding the ADA. As you will see, these responsibilities are wide-ranging.

Often our challenges as individuals on the spectrum are invisible to others. This can lead to misunderstanding and a kind of involuntary discrimination. For example, a woman with Asperger Syndrome once boarded a bus during rush hour in New York City. In order to pay her fare, she had to insert a prepaid card into a small machine located near the bus driver. The woman had spatial and visual processing challenges and, therefore, had to make several attempts to insert her card into the apparatus. The machine would only accept the card if the electronic stripe was inserted in the correct direction and if the card itself was face up. Each time she tried, the woman inserted it the wrong way. The bus driver became impatient, as did several passengers on the bus. No one stepped forward to assist her. Instead, some passengers raised their voices or yelled that she should get off the bus. Even the bus driver became angry. No one knew she was an individual with autism. Had she been in a wheelchair or been blind, the passengers would not have dared raise a voice, and the bus driver would have accommodated her immediately. This is because our culture is more immediately informed about the needs for accommodation of individuals who are blind or have mobility differences. In fact, within the disability movement itself, autistic people arrived at their own voice as self-advocates much later than those of other groups, such as the deaf or the blind communities.

The ADA provides that individuals with disabilities must receive equal access to public transportation. Luckily, the woman with Asperger Syndrome who attempted to board the bus knew her rights and disclosed to the bus driver that she had a disability. Immediately, he assisted her by modeling how to insert the fare card properly. She was then able to take a seat on the bus. Stories like this abound in our autism community. In some instances, the outcome is not as positive as it was for the woman on the bus. For example, many adults with autism have stories of being denied employment or the opportunity to attend college or graduate school because of their differences. The ADA is a comprehensive law that prohibits this kind discrimination, but as you can see, sometimes we must assert our own voices and educate others in order to be treated with the dignity and fairness that are our right.

In many respects, the ADA is an extension of the Civil Rights Act of 1964, which made discrimination based on race, religion, sex, and national origin illegal. In the mid-1960s, our society had not evolved enough to include individuals with disabilities in this important legislation. Because our history includes an unfortunate legacy of second-class citizenship, it has reinforced (for some of us) the misinformed notion that we may not enjoy the same legal rights as our fellow citizens. This has to do with a long history of being perceived as outsiders, burdens to society, or citizens less worthy of basic human and civil rights. Today, with the ADA enacted, any change in our quality of life must, therefore, come both from without and from within ourselves. Knowing your rights will serve you well in many situations, and remember, as you assert your own rights, you are also contributing to greater awareness in the general population. Those who follow in your path will reap the benefits of your having voiced your rights, asserted your needs, and demanded equal opportunity and respect in the country you live in.

The ADA is broken down into five sections or "titles." These include the following categories of legal protection: 1) Employment, 2) Public Services, 3) Public Accommodations, 4) Telecommunications, and 5) Miscellaneous Provisions. On the next page is a self-test for you to complete. By working through this quiz, you will learn more about each title of the ADA. Keep in mind that the ADA is a complex document. The information in this unit is by no means exhaustive, but it will provide a foundation for understanding how the ADA works in your life. If you would like to learn more, you can visit the official ADA web site at www.ada.gov.

AMERICANS WITH DISABILITIES ACT	
Words or Phrases	**Definitions and Notes**

Self-Test on the Americans with Disabilities Act (ADA)

Below are simple true/false questions that are meant to get you thinking about the various ways that the ADA protects your civil rights. It's O.K. if you don't know the answers. The self-test is meant to provide scenarios where ADA plays an important role and to increase your awareness of its presence in day-to-day life.

1. Title I of the ADA states that employers may not discriminate against individuals with disabilities.

True or false: During a job interview, an employer may ask you if you are disabled and require information about the specifics of your disability. Even if you're capable of doing the job, the employer may exclude you from the pool of candidates because of your disability.

☐ True   ☐ False

2. Title II of the ADA covers various aspects of public services and transportation provided by public entities, including access. The title specifically states that public transit entities may not deny access to individuals with disabilities.

True or false: A woman with Asperger Syndrome may not board a bus operated by her municipality if her visual-processing challenges make it difficult for her to insert her electronic card into the machine that accepts payment for the fare.

☐ True   ☐ False

3. Title III deals with public accommodations, including commercial facilities (such as stores, places of lodging, education, transportation and more). In this section, the ADA ensures that individuals with disabilities may enjoy the goods, services, facilities or accommodations of public places.

True or false: A man with mobility challenges uses a wheel chair to get around. He wants to go to a movie. It's O.K. for the movie theater to refuse selling him a ticket because his wheelchair is too big and might disturb the other visitors to the theater.

☐ True   ☐ False

4.   Title IV requires all telecommunications companies to ensure functionally equivalent services for customers with disabilities, particularly the deaf, the hard of hearing or those with speech differences.

True of false: An autistic man who has challenges speaking but likes to type may receive special services from his phone company in order to type his conversations with others rather than talking.

☐   True   ☐   False

5.   Title V of the ADA covers miscellaneous items. One important element of this section is the anti-retaliation or coercion provision. To give you a sense of the language of the ADA, here is a quote from this title:

Individuals who exercise their rights under the ADA, or assist others in exercising their rights, are protected from retaliation. The prohibition against retaliation or coercion applies broadly to any individual or entity that seeks to prevent an individual from exercising his or her rights or to retaliate against him or her for having exercised those rights … Any form of retaliation or coercion, including threats, intimidation, or interference, is prohibited if it is intended to interfere with the exercise of rights under the ADA.

This provision means that when you attempt to assert your rights under the Americans with Disabilities Act, others are not allowed to interfere or threaten you for doing so.

True or false: When the passengers on the bus insisted that the woman with Asperger Syndrome get off because she was having trouble with her fare card, they were infringing on her civil rights.

☐   True   ☐   False

Answer Key:
1. False   2. False   3. False   4. True   5. True

B. Extended Lesson: Crossword Puzzle

Across

1. Unfair treatment of one person or group because of prejudice about race, ethnic group age, religion, gender, or disability

2. Something that is handed down or remains from a previous generation or time

3. To make proposed legislation into law

4. The process of writing and passing laws

Down

1. A medically diagnosed condition that makes it difficult to engage in the activities of daily life

5. An official command or instruction from an authority

6. A division of a law, statute or law book

7. Acronym for an important civil rights act passed in 1990

Answer Key:

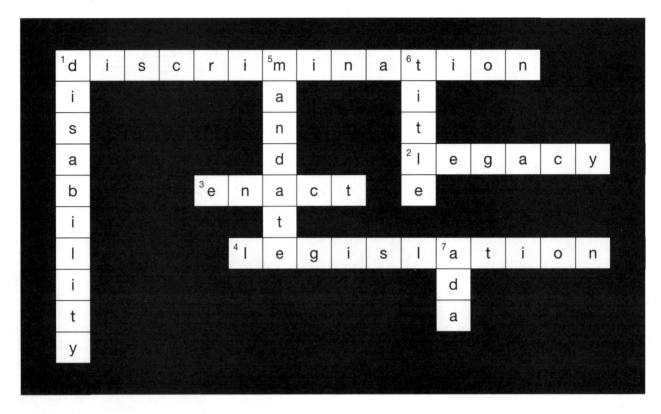

Self-Advocacy Portfolio

Introduction

The *Self-Advocacy Portfolio* is the backbone of the Integrated Self-Advocacy ISA system. Unlike the other units of the curriculum, the portfolio extends beyond classroom lessons and therapeutic activities into everyday, real-life experiences and situations for the individual with autism. This is where advocacy learning is translated into practice. Although you will find no lesson plans here, the *Self-Advocacy Portfolio* does aim to cover important objectives:

- To provide students with a central location for documenting, reviewing, and updating successful advocacy strategies
- To validate students' development in a format that can be shared with friends, family, mentors, support people, professionals, therapists, employers, physicians, and teachers
- To serve as a living document that has the capacity and flexibility to accompany the individual with autism through a variety of settings and life changes
- To provide helpful information to schools and other state and federal programs that wish to document progress on goals, fortify the IEP or ISP, author meaningful transition plans, or provide evidence for best practices.

How to Use the Portfolio

The *Self-Advocacy Portfolio* consists of six sections. Many of the sections are associated directly with specific units of *The Integrated Self-Advocacy ISA Curriculum*. This structure assists students in creating, organizing, and updating their advocacy strategies on an ongoing basis. Any time students see the familiar portfolio icon Ⓟ in their Student Workbooks or on worksheets they are completing, they will know it's time to transfer specific unit information they have gathered to the *Self-Advocacy Portfolio* for further development and safe keeping.

Below are descriptions of the core components of the *Self-Advocacy Portfolio*. They will help you understand how to navigate the curriculum while making maximum use of all the amazing things the portfolio has to offer.

From Paradiz, V. (2009). *The Integrated Self-Advocacy ISA™ Curriculum – A Program for Emerging Self-Advocates with Autism Spectrum and Other Conditions.* Autism Asperger Publishing Company; www.asperger.net. Used with permission.

My Advocacy Scripts

The Advocacy Scripts section is directly associated with Unit 3 of *The Integrated Self-Advocacy ISA Curriculum*, *Getting Our Words and Thoughts Out*. This lesson offers insight into the challenges in discourse that individuals with ASD can have and assists students in understanding the difference between effective and ineffective advocacy strategies. The lesson worksheet, Making an Advocacy Script, cues students to gather all the information needed to author a verbal script they can use (speak, program into a communication device, etc.) to advocate for a specific need or preference. With this information in hand, students come here, to the *Self-Advocacy Portfolio*, to write and file the script, so that it is ready to use and easy to access in one location.

My Advocacy Action Plans

The Advocacy Plans section is associated primarily with two units of the curriculum, *The Sensory Scan* (Unit 4) and *The Social Scan* (Unit 6). Using the Scan worksheets in these units, students conduct surveys of environments in order to discover their sensory and social needs, preferences, or discomforts specific to a given setting. Students then bring the results of their scans to the *Self-Advocacy Portfolio* to develop, document, and archive their Advocacy Action Plans. Finally, additional Advocacy Plans can be developed based on lesson plans teachers or therapists have written and taught themselves using the Integrated Self-Advocacy ISA Lesson Planning Template located in the Appendix on pages 137-139.

My Individualized Education Program (IEP)

The IEP section is used as a repository for IEP statements that students develop as a result of completing the two worksheets in Unit 10, *Becoming a Part of Your IEP*. Here, students file or update statements they have written for attending these important meetings.

Notes for My Transition Plan or My Individual Service Plan (ISP)

This section is a resource for students, families, schools, or agencies that wish to author or enhance meaningful transition plans or Individual Service Plans (ISP). Materials derived from student projects and activities, ranging from successful advocacy strategies to possible career directions, are documented here and can be integrated into these important planning documents.

From Paradiz, V. (2009). *The Integrated Self-Advocacy ISA™ Curriculum – A Program for Emerging Self-Advocates with Autism Spectrum and Other Conditions.* Autism Asperger Publishing Company; www.asperger.net. Used with permission.

My Favorite Advocacy Resources, Support People, and Mentors

This section gives students a place to assemble important resources they turn to regularly in their lives as self-advocates, including support people, Web-related resources, organizations, and peer groups.

My Articles, Commentaries, and Reflections on Topics in Self-Advocacy

Here students assemble essays or other projects they have created in the course of completing *The Integrated Self-Advocacy ISA Curriculum*. This is the place for saving favorite articles, reports, or writings they have generated from the Self-Reflection portion of each unit. Students are also provided with guidelines for submitting articles and commentaries on topics involving autism to the editors of the Integrated Self-Advocacy ISA web site where they can be considered for publication.

To submit, go to www.valerieparadiz.com/community.

 Remember, you can offer students the option of using electronic versions of the worksheets and the **Self-Advocacy Portfolio** *provided on the CD that accompanies this book. Many students with autism spectrum and related conditions can perform better when given the option of working on a computer.*

My Self-Advocacy Portfolio

_____

Name

Table of Contents

Introduction

Welcome to your *Self-Advocacy Portfolio*, your home away from home! We'd like you to think of your portfolio as if it were a safe haven or a loyal friend who is always there for you when you need a voice or must find a way to fulfill your needs or solve problems.

As your portfolio grows – as you fill it with information and insights about yourself – you will begin to see that you are on an exciting journey of self-discovery! With time, you will have tools and strategies for becoming more independent and effective in your day-to-day interactions with environments and people, and these tools will be tailored specifically to who you are. And if you discover something along the way that you would like to share with others in the autism community, the editors of the Integrated Self-Advocacy ISA web site (www.valerieparadiz.com/community) invite you to submit articles, commentaries, and letters to be considered for publication. Enjoy using your portfolio!

From Paradiz, V. (2009). *The Integrated Self-Advocacy ISA™ Curriculum – A Program for Emerging Self-Advocates with Autism Spectrum and Other Conditions.* Autism Asperger Publishing Company; www.asperger.net. Used with permission.

My Advocacy Scripts

In Unit 3, *Getting Our Words and Thoughts Out*, you learned how to write your own advocacy script using the Making an Advocacy Script worksheet. This is the place where you can archive scripts that have worked well for you, so that you can use them again in the future or show others how helpful they are to you. All you need to do is record information for each script below. They will be here for you whenever you need to remember them, adapt them, or share them.

Remember that every time you advocate for yourself, you are in an original moment in your life. Although you have prepared your scripts and have imagined how you would like things to go when you use them, you might not get the results you want, or the words you are prepared to say, sign, or input into your communication device might be understood differently than you intended, depending on the context.

In any advocacy moment, it's important to keep an open mind and to *expect* that things won't always go the way you want them to. Advocacy is an ongoing process. The success is in attempting it!

From Paradiz, V. (2009). *The Integrated Self-Advocacy ISA™ Curriculum – A Program for Emerging Self-Advocates with Autism Spectrum and Other Conditions.* Autism Asperger Publishing Company; www.asperger.net. Used with permission.

My Advocacy Scripts

Scripts *Write out the script you created using the Making an Advocacy Script worksheet*	Where I Used This Script	When I Used This Script	Rating: How did it go? 1 poorly 2 O.K. (didn't reach goal) 3 O.K. (reached part of goal) 4 great!

From Paradiz, V. (2009). *The Integrated Self-Advocacy ISA™ Curriculum – A Program for Emerging Self-Advocates with Autism Spectrum and Other Conditions.* Autism Asperger Publishing Company; www.asperger.net. Used with permission.

My Advocacy Action Plans

In Units 4 and 6 you conducted scans to collect information about your sensory and social needs, preferences, or discomforts specific to a setting, such as a classroom, where you work, or somewhere in the community. Here is where you can use that information to create a plan of action for increasing your comfort or feeling of autonomy in that setting or environment. Find the category of plan you will write below (a: sensory/environmental, b: social, or c: other) in the graphs on pages 121-123, and follow the steps provided. Remember to rate your Advocacy Plan after you have tested it out. You can always make changes to the plan if you want to use it again in the future, or adapt it to new situations.

Before you start working on your Advocacy Plans, please take a moment to read and think about the advocacy tips on the following page.

From Paradiz, V. (2009). *The Integrated Self-Advocacy ISA™ Curriculum – A Program for Emerging Self-Advocates with Autism Spectrum and Other Conditions.* Autism Asperger Publishing Company; www.asperger.net. Used with permission.

Advocacy Tips from Stephen Shore, Ed.D.

Maximize your chances for success when planning your advocacy efforts by considering the following "wh" questions before your initial communication.

A. *Whom* are you going to talk to? Usually it will be the person you have most of your contact with. For example, in a work situation, you will probably talk to your immediate supervisor. In grade school, you likely will start with your aide, if you have one, or your teacher.

B. *When* are you going to make your advocacy effort? Plan for when the person you talk to is not busy or otherwise distracted. When possible, make an appointment to speak with that person in advance. Whether the time has been decided in advance or the advocacy effort is more spontaneous, *always* precede your conversation by asking, "Is this a good time for us to talk?"

C. *Why* are you asking for a modification, accommodation, or greater understanding at this time? The Sensory and Social Scans will be helpful in answering these questions. Some examples may relate to greater productivity at work or address visual or other sensory sensitivities.

D. *What* are you asking for?

An *accommodation* is asking for a change in how things are done so that you may achieve your objective in school, work, or some other situation. Examples include a change in the type of lighting or a difference in how a test is presented in school, such as verbally instead of written.

A *modification* is asking for a change in expectations. Some examples include a reduced number of bicycles assembled per day at work or reducing the number of questions on a test.

Greater *understanding* helps the other person realize how things are for you in a given situation. For example, a person with extreme hearing sensitivities may explain to her coworker that tapping her fingers on the desk sounds like a machine gun, and therefore is very distracting.

It's likely that you will use more than one or even all of these categories in a single advocacy effort.

It will be helpful if you role-play your advocacy effort with a trusted person such as a friend, parent, mentor, or other safe individual.

It is not always necessary to advocate verbally. Some people may find greater success communicating via written letter, e-mail, instant message, recorded statement, or other assistive communication device.

From Paradiz, V. (2009). *The Integrated Self-Advocacy ISA™ Curriculum – A Program for Emerging Self-Advocates with Autism Spectrum and Other Conditions.* Autism Asperger Publishing Company; www.asperger.net. Used with permission.

A. Sensory and Environmental Advocacy Plans

My top 3 sensory needs *Transfer this information from your Sensory Scan worksheet*	Can I address these sensory needs on my own? If so, how? *For example, do you need tools, such as fidgets, earplugs, or sunglasses?*	If I can't address these sensory needs on my own, what is my advocacy goal? *For example, do you need to make a request for an accommodation?*	Do I need an Advocacy Script? *If yes, complete an Advocacy Script worksheet from Unit 3, and enter your script here.*	Do I need someone to support me? If so, how? *You might want to practice your plan first, ask someone to accompany you, or follow up with a mentor after you have executed your Advocacy Plan.*	Rating: How did it go? 1 2 3 poorly O.K. great!

From Paradiz, V. (2009). *The Integrated Self-Advocacy ISA™ Curriculum – A Program for Emerging Self-Advocates with Autism Spectrum and Other Conditions.* Autism Asperger Publishing Company; www.asperger.net. Used with permission.

B. Social Advocacy Plans

My social discomforts and tendencies *Transfer this information from your Social Scan worksheet*	Can I address my social needs on my own? If so, how? *For example, do you need to spend less time in this environment, can you take breaks or do an activity that will help structure your experience more?*	If I can't address my social needs on my own, what is my advocacy goal? *For example, do you need to make a request for a modification or for assistance of some kind?*	Do I need an Advocacy Script? *If yes, complete an Advocacy Script worksheet from Unit 3, and enter your script below.*	Do I need someone to support me? If so, how? *You might want to practice your plan first, ask someone to accompany you, or follow up with a mentor after you have executed your Advocacy Plan.*	Rating: How did it go? 1 unbearable 2 uncomfortable 3 not a problem 4 comfortable!

C. Additional Advocacy Plans

My advocacy goal	Do I need an advocacy script? If yes, complete an Advocacy Script Worksheet from Unit 3 and enter your script below.	Do I need someone to support me? If so, how? You might want to practice your plan first, ask someone to accompany you, or follow up with a mentor after you have executed your Advocacy Plan.	Rating: How did it go? 1 2 3 poorly O.K. great!

My Individualized Education Program (IEP)

This section is where you can file and update statements you have written based on the lesson activities in Unit 10, *Becoming a Part of Your IEP.* In that unit, two worksheets, Exploring IEP Options and Writing an IEP Statement, guided you through a process of deciding how you want to participate in your IEP meeting and what you wish to share with others attending that meeting. Keep any plans for how you will participate and statements you write here, so that you can turn to them again in the future.

Date of IEP Meeting	How I Will Participate	My Statement

Notes for My Transition Plan or My Individual Service Plan (ISP)

If you are a high school student, or if you are an adult receiving services through programs in your state, you can keep important notes here to share with teachers, therapists, administrators, case managers, or support providers. Your notes are meant to give the people who support you now (or who will support you in the near future) background information on the things in your life that are important to you, particularly career directions you would like to explore or become trained in and advocacy plans that you have developed and would like to use after you leave school, move to a new home, or start a new job. You can also keep general notes on your social tendencies and your environmental and sensory needs here, since these are important factors in ensuring your well-being at home, school or college, work, and in the community. When you share this information with support people in schools and programs, they can integrate it into the services they provide you with, giving you a chance to have your own voice and input in these very important processes!

A. Career Directions and Training

In Unit 7, *Cultivating Strengths and Focused Interests*, you explored various career directions, arriving at a top career choice using the worksheet called Focused Interests and Careers. If you would like state agencies, school personnel, or others who support you to assist you in finding opportunities to learn more about this career or gain more training and experience, write your top choice in the space provided on the following page, then answer the remaining questions.

If you have discovered another career direction that you did not investigate in Unit 7 but would like to, feel free to explore it here. Or, if you have a variety of interests, complete additional surveys. Remember, choosing a field to explore doesn't mean you must commit to it for life! It's always good to think through a variety of possibilities, imagine yourself doing them, and get a sense of the training or education you'll need in order to do them. If you give yourself a chance to investigate in this way, you're more likely to move in directions that are best suited to your personality, interests, and abilities.

If you can't answer all the questions in the surveys, ask your teacher, therapist, or someone in your family to help you.

From Paradiz, V. (2009). *The Integrated Self-Advocacy ISA™ Curriculum – A Program for Emerging Self-Advocates with Autism Spectrum and Other Conditions.* Autism Asperger Publishing Company; www.asperger.net. Used with permission.

My Top Career Choice *Transfer your career choice from the Focused Interests and Careers worksheet or write in a new one.*	Required Training or Education	Sensory or Social Challenges I Might Have on the Job	Accommodations or Modifications I Might Make or Request to Do This Job Well	Prior Experience I Have Had in This Field or a Related Field

My Top Career Choice	Required Training or Education	Sensory or Social Challenges I Might Have on the Job	Accommodations or Modifications I Might Make or Request to Do This Job Well	Prior Experience I Have Had in This Field or a Related Field

My Top Career Choice	Required Training or Education	Sensory or Social Challenges I Might Have on the Job	Accommodations or Modifications I Might Make or Request to Do This Job Well	Prior Experience I Have Had in This Field or a Related Field

My Top Career Choice	Required Training or Education	Sensory or Social Challenges I Might Have on the Job	Accommodations or Modifications I Might Make or Request to Do This Job Well	Prior Experience I Have Had in This Field or a Related Field

From Paradiz, V. (2009). *The Integrated Self-Advocacy ISA™ Curriculum – A Program for Emerging Self-Advocates with Autism Spectrum and Other Conditions.* Autism Asperger Publishing Company; www.asperger.net. Used with permission.

B. My Favorite Advocacy Plans

Review the Advocacy Action Plans you have recorded in this *Self-Advocacy Portfolio*. Are there any plans you have found extremely useful? Are there some that you can imagine using in other contexts or settings, if you were to start a new job, for instance, or move into a house alone or with other roommates? What about being in new places in the community? If so, make note of your favorite or most effective plans here, so that others who support you know that they should integrate them into your service, school or employment program.

C. My Sensory and Social Profile

In Units 4 and 6, you learned a lot about yourself by conducting Sensory and Social Scans. Now that you have more experience conducting scans and advocating for your needs and preferences, can you offer general comments about your social tendencies or environmental needs? These would include needs that are relatively consistent for you day-to-day. For example, loud thunder might make you feel anxious any time it happens. This is something good for others to know about. Or you might know that you always feel unable to speak when you're in a crowded room, compared to talking to someone one on one. The spaces on the following page allow you to share some of your most specific needs with others, things you have learned about yourself and know that if others understood them, you'd generally be happier and more comfortable. If you have trouble filling in this section, you can always review your Sensory and Social Scans and look for the things that are most important to your comfort and then transfer that information here.

From Paradiz, V. (2009). *The Integrated Self-Advocacy ISA™ Curriculum – A Program for Emerging Self-Advocates with Autism Spectrum and Other Conditions.* Autism Asperger Publishing Company; www.asperger.net. Used with permission.

D. My Sensory Needs and Tendencies

E. My Social Needs and Tendencies

My Favorite Advocacy Resources, Support People, and Mentors

Now that you have become a "pro" in self-advocacy, you might want to take a moment to remember the helpful support people, mentors, and resources that have assisted you in this process. It's a good idea to keep track of the people and resources that play an important role in your happiness and comfort day-to-day. You can share this information with others who are just getting to know you, for example. Or you can keep track of contact information, links on the web, or other information and have it all in one place in case you need it again.

Name of Support Person, Organization, Group, or Resource	Contact Information, Address, Telephone Number, Web Links, Email Address	How This Person, Organization, or Resource Has Supported Me in Becoming a Self-Advocate

My Articles, Commentaries, and Reflections on Topics in Self-Advocacy

Several of the units in this book have involved creating reports or writing essays. In other instances, you have been invited to think about specific questions in the Self-Reflection sections of the units. This portion of your *Self-Advocacy Portfolio* is the place where you can save your favorite commentaries and reflections in one place, so that others who read this can learn more about you and your thoughts regarding the autism community.

The editors of the Integrated Self-Advocacy ISA web site would also like to invite you to submit your favorite writings for possible publication. Though we cannot promise to publish every submission, we encourage you to send us your thoughts and reports! Submission guidelines are simple. Send us up to 1,000 words (maximum) in a Word document. You can find out more by visiting www.valerieparadiz.com/community.

From Paradiz, V. (2009). *The Integrated Self-Advocacy ISA™ Curriculum – A Program for Emerging Self-Advocates with Autism Spectrum and Other Conditions.* Autism Asperger Publishing Company; www.asperger.net. Used with permission.

Appendix

Where Can I Use This Curriculum?

The Integrated Self-Advocacy ISA Curriculum is designed for a variety of settings in schools and organizations. Here are a few examples:

- Classrooms
- Group or individual counseling
- Social skills class or group
- Therapeutic settings, such as OT or speech/language
- In-home instruction
- After-school or community programs
- ASD programs for college students or young adults
- Residential settings
- ASD peer support groups
- Mentoring or coaching
- Transition preparedness

If you are a teacher working in a middle- or high-school setting wondering how on earth you can fit this curriculum into your already busy academic schedule, you might integrate Units 2 and 5, which discuss the Autism Community and the History of Autism, into a health class. Unit 7, which is devoted to identifying and fostering strengths and focused interests, can be utilized for a home and careers class, while Unit 8, which explores historical role models with autism, or Unit 11, which introduces students to the Americans with Disabilities Act, can be easily integrated into history or social studies classes.

If you are working in a group therapy setting or teaching in an ASD classroom, you may wish to offer *all* the units to the class as a segment of the social skills curriculum. For high-school and college students, you can think about offering the curriculum as an independent study, placing emphasis on the writing assignments.

Finally, you might consider using portions of this curriculum for *all* your students with special needs, regardless of their diagnoses or classifications. It is highly adaptable and useful in preparing students for IEP meetings, creating transition plans with student involvement, and providing evidence and documentation on student goals and progress.

If you are a case manager, therapist, or supervisor of an adult program or residence, you might consider using the curriculum to support the adults in your care in expanding their experience of self-awareness, autonomy, and competence in their daily environments of home, work and community. You can also turn to the *Self-Advocacy Portfolio* for important information when it's time to write or review the ISP, while fulfilling person-centered objectives of your organization.

General Suggestions for Adapting Lessons

Below are a few general suggestions for adapting the lessons. Unlike the suggestions you'll find at key points throughout the book, the list below offers pointers that are less specific to the content and more applicable universally to all lessons.

- Simplify the lesson by reading essay segments aloud to students.
- In a therapeutic situation, read aloud or take turns reading with a student or a small group of students.
- If a student has difficulty reading and processing the unit essays, use a silent timer and allow for shorter reading periods of 2-5 minutes. When the student has read for the allotted amount of time, he/she may get up and move around for 1-2 minutes, returning again to his/her seat for more reading.
- If students are practicing note-taking skills, build in time for them to copy definitions of new vocabulary and important concepts from the board into the space provided in their Student Workbooks.
- Provide additional visual supports for all lessons as needed.

For Nonverbal Students or Individuals Communicating with Devices, Sign Language, or Other Means

Although *The Integrated Self-Advocacy ISA Curriculum* has not been fully developed for nonverbal individuals or for those on the spectrum who are not in the same cognitive range as individuals with Asperger Syndrome and high-functioning autism, some units can be adapted for these populations. For example, in a pilot program in the New York City's School District 75, nonverbal and cognitively challenged high-school students in a self-contained special education classroom learned about the sensory systems and how to conduct Sensory Scans using *The Integrated Self-Advocacy ISA Curriculum*. The classroom teacher adapted the readings of Unit 4, *The Social Scan*, using an image-based reading system, additional behavioral supports, and modified scan worksheets. For updates and future publications specific to this population of individuals on the spectrum, be sure to visit the Integrated Self-Advocacy ISA web site at www.valerieparadiz.com/community.

The Benefits of Teaching Self-Advocacy Skills

In the pilot program noted above, a nonverbal student was taught how to use the Sensory Scan to advocate for environmental accommodations. As the student became more adept at scanning and creating successful advocacy action plans, both aggressive and interruptive behaviors decreased significantly, as illustrated in the following graph.

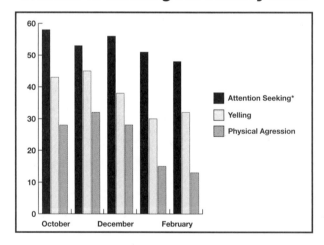

Benefits of Learning the Sensory Scan

Such data indicate that as students gain greater sensory self-awareness, they can learn to identify their environmental triggers and act more proactively in challenging environments. In some instances, what we often call "behaviors" might be viewed alternatively as ineffective advocacy strategies. Guiding students toward effective strategies by providing lessons and experiences that assist them in discovering their advocacy ability can have tremendous results, enhancing their quality of life, self-esteem, and independence.

Write an Original Lesson Plan to Teach Self-Advocacy Skills

As you become familiar with *The Integrated Self-Advocacy ISA Curriculum*, you might begin to identify additional learning goals for your students that are not covered in the curriculum units. Below is a template that guides you through a six-step process for writing your own lesson plan geared toward fostering self-advocacy. Before you write your own plan, it might be helpful to keep a few things in mind:

- **Identify a Viable Self-Advocacy Goal**

  Identifying a *genuine* lesson goal is critical. Avoid turning to IEP goals, social skills goals, or other therapeutic goals unless you feel they truly support a student in moving toward greater self-determination and independence. Sometimes this means letting go of some of our authority (or possibly our overly controlling presence) in a classroom setting; at other times, it might simply mean putting IEP or other goals on the back burner just to see what happens. After you have implemented the lesson, you might even discover that some of the goals are addressed in ways you had never intended. The important thing is to not let externally determined therapeutic or academic goals drive the lesson, but rather the individual self-advocacy needs of the student.

- **Assess for Indicators of Self-Determination**

  One way to be sure the lesson goal is in keeping with the principles of self-determination theory is to look for important indicators. Does the lesson or goal you have in mind provide the individual or your students with experiences through which they can gain greater self-awareness, autonomy, or competence in advocating for their needs, accommodations, and preferences? By taking a short moment to review these points and make notes, you can assess whether the goal you have in mind is relevant to self-advocacy.

- **Identify and Incorporate Intrinsic and/or Extrinsic Motivations**

  Before you write the lesson plan, consider incorporating or making note of the intrinsic and extrinsic motivations that might become a part of your lesson plan or play a role during implementation.

  Intrinsic motivations are activities that people do naturally and spontaneously when they feel free to follow their interests. For example, if you were to walk into a room full of children carrying a bottle of soap bubbles with a wand and then went on to blow bubbles into the air, many children would likely run after the bubbles in spontaneous glee. For individuals with autism, deep and focused interests are sometimes intrinsic motivators. As you write the lesson plan, consider whether building in such a motivator will assist you and the student in achieving the self-advocacy goal.

Extrinsic motivations, on the other hand, don't arise in a natural, spontaneous way within the individual. Instead, these motivations tend to be dictated by external factors, such as social pressures, cultural values, or behavioral expectations. This is a significant realm of life that individuals on the spectrum find challenging, and quite often, our therapeutic or learning goals for them are derived from these very external factors. For example, learning good hygiene habits, such as how to brush one's teeth (and carry through doing it on a daily basis) involves a number of extrinsic motivators. The ultimate benefit is clear: increased health and greater social integration. However, compared to an intrinsic motivation, the extrinsic does not happen naturally or spontaneously. One eventually learns to feel motivated to brush one's teeth, but it takes some time to integrate this.

As you write a lesson plan that aims to teach a self-advocacy skill, it is a good idea to think through what extrinsic motivations will be involved in implementing the lesson and actually achieving the lesson goal. If too many such demands are placed on the student, you might consider eliminating some of them, or balancing them with the introduction of an intrinsic motivator to ensure success.

Share Your Ideas with Your Educational and Therapeutic Community!

If you write a lesson plan that you would like to share with colleagues who are also working toward the goal of greater self-determination or person-centered planning, we invite you to submit your commentaries, case studies, or sample lesson plans to the editors of the Integrated Self-Advocacy ISA web site. Please limit your submission to 1,000 words. For more information, visit www.valerieparadiz.com/community.

You can also visit the web site to learn more tips and strategies from your colleagues, students on the autism spectrum and the self-advocacy community! We hope to see you there!

Self-Advocacy Lesson Planning
Integrated Self-Advocacy ISA™

Step 1:	Identify Goal
Step 2:	List Self-Determination Indicators
Step 3:	Identify Intrinsic/Extrinsic Motivations

Your name: _____ Date: _____

1. Identify a Self-Advocacy Goal

In one or two sentences, describe the goal of self-advocacy.

2. List Self-Determination Indicators

Which of the following indicators of self-determination are involved in working toward this goal?

		How are they involved? Make your notes here.
Self-Awareness:	☐ yes ☐ no	
Autonomy:	☐ yes ☐ no	
Competence:	☐ yes ☐ no	

3. Identify Intrinsic and Extrinsic Motivations

In the lesson plan you are about to write, you might choose to incorporate an individual's intrinsic motivations (favorite stims or a deep interest). Extrinsic motivations may or may not be part of the plan. Extrinsic motivations don't come from the individual, but from the environment and cultural expectations around the individual.

Intrinsic Motivation(s)	Notes
Extrinsic Motivation(s)	Notes

Consider the strengths and weaknesses of incorporating these motivations into the lesson plan. Will they support the individual in moving to new experiences of self-awareness, autonomy, or competence through self-advocacy?

List Lesson Plan Team Members: _____ Location of Lesson: _____

Today's Date: _____ Date(s) of Lesson Implementation: _____ Team Review Date: _____

From Paradiz, V. (2009). *The Integrated Self-Advocacy ISA™ Curriculum – A Program for Emerging Self-Advocates with Autism Spectrum and Other Conditions*. Autism Asperger Publishing Company; www.asperger.net. Used with permission.

Self-Advocacy Lesson Planning
Integrated Self-Advocacy ISA™

Step 4: Write Lesson Plan
Step 5: Implement Lesson
Step 6: Conduct Assessment

Self-Advocacy Lesson Planning

4. Write the Lesson Plan

Name and Brief Description of the Lesson Plan:

Date the Lesson Will Be Implemented:

Self-Advocacy Goal:

Intrinsic/Extrinsic Motivations:

Teaching Supports:
List the types of supports that will be used in implementing the lesson (visual supports, picture exchange, Time Timer, sign language, audio or video enhancements, keyboard devices, etc.)

Materials Needed:

6. Conduct Assessment

Would you use this lesson again? In what context?

Was the self-advocacy goal met? (circle)
yes   partially   no

Was incorporation of motivations supportive to the student in learning the self-advocacy skill?
yes   partially   no

If extrinsic motivations were involved, which degree of motivation did you observe?
☐ unwillingness
☐ passive compliance
☐ active personal commitment

Did you use the supports you had intended to?
yes   partially   no

List any supports that need further refinement.

List any supports you hadn't planned on using, but proved to be useful.

Were the materials adequate/appropriate? If not, how could they be improved?

Self-Advocacy Lesson Planning
Integrated Self-Advocacy ISA™

Step 4: Write Lesson Plan
Step 5: Implement Lesson
Step 6: Conduct Assessment

5. Implement the Lesson: Activity → Teaching Strategies → Name of Person Leading Activity
Divide the lesson into discrete activities, describing each step deliberately. Next to the activity description, list the specific teaching strategies you will use and clearly indicate who will take the lead if you are team teaching.

ACTIVITY	TEACHING STRATEGIES	LEAD

On a scale from 1 to 5, how do you feel about the lesson overall (1 = "it was a disaster and no goals were met," 5 = "it went perfectly, and we met all our goals"):

1   2   3   4   5

Other Comments:

Planning Checklist:
___ Will you make use of the *Self-Advocacy Portfolio* in this lesson plan. If so, how?
___ Did you include specific teaching strategies and a leader for each activity?
___ Did you incorporate the intrinsic and/or extrinsic motivations you had intended to?

From Paradiz, V. (2009). *The Integrated Self-Advocacy ISA™ Curriculum – A Program for Emerging Self-Advocates with Autism Spectrum and Other Conditions.* Autism Asperger Publishing Company; www.asperger.net. Used with permission.

Let's Work Together

Directions for How to Be an Effective and Supportive Team Member

1. Make sure each team member has a clearly defined job to do. If you are not certain what your role is, make sure to get support in defining it.

2. Don't do other members' jobs. Remember, when you work in a team, everyone participates. If you interrupt or offer too much input, others might not be participating as much as they would like to.

3. Make suggestions politely, rather than bossing or telling someone else what to do. When making a suggestion, you can say:
   "I'd like to suggest that we …," or
   "I have another possible way of looking at it …," or
   "What if we were to try …"

   This is how you offer constructive suggestions rather than critical remarks. This is a good thing to practice with your classmates because you need to know how to do team work and cooperate with others in many situations in life.

   Also, when you make a suggestion, always be prepared for various outcomes (rather than what you wish or imagine will happen). For example:
   a) Your suggestion might get adopted by the group.
   b) You suggestion might get turned down.
   c) A portion of your suggestion might be accepted or adapted.

4. Allow the group to vote on decisions that aren't getting unanimous support from each member. Everyone must agree to accept the vote, so that you can move on to the next step in the project.

5. Allow all members to process information at their own pace. This shows respect for your fellow classmates.

6. Offer each other positive support. You can say:

   "That's was really terrific how you…," or
   "I like your ideas!" or
   "You're an important part of this project! Thank you!"

7. Don't say critical things to one another, since this only slows down the process and makes others feel unhappy and unable to work as a team.

Advocacy Tips from Stephen Shore, Ed.D.

Maximize your chances for success when planning your advocacy efforts by considering the following "wh" questions before your initial communication.

A. *Whom* are you going to talk to? Usually it will be the person you have most of your contact with. For example, in a work situation, you will probably talk to your immediate supervisor. In grade school, you likely will start with your aide, if you have one, or your teacher.

B. *When* are you going to make your advocacy effort? Plan for when the person you talk to is not busy or otherwise distracted. When possible, make an appointment to speak with that person in advance. Whether the time has been decided in advance or the advocacy effort is more spontaneous, *always* precede your conversation by asking, "Is this a good time for us to talk?"

C. *Why* are you asking for a modification, accommodation, or greater understanding at this time? The Sensory and Social Scans will be helpful in answering these questions. Some examples may relate to greater productivity at work or address visual or other sensory sensitivities.

D. *What* are you asking for?

An *accommodation* is asking for a change in how things are done so that you may achieve your objective in school, work, or some other situation. Examples include a change in the type of lighting or a difference in how a test is presented in school, such as verbally instead of written.

A *modification* is asking for a change in expectations. Some examples include a reduced number of bicycles assembled per day at work or reducing the number of questions on a test.

Greater *understanding* helps the other person realize how things are for you in a given situation. For example, a person with extreme hearing sensitivities may explain to her coworker that tapping her fingers on the desk sounds like a machine gun, and therefore is very distracting.

It's likely that you will use more than one or even all of these categories in a single advocacy effort.

It will be helpful if you role-play your advocacy effort with a trusted person such as a friend, parent, mentor, or other safe individual.

It is not always necessary to advocate verbally. Some people may find greater success communicating via written letter, e-mail, instant message, recorded statement, or other assistive communication device.

From Paradiz, V. (2009). *The Integrated Self-Advocacy ISA™ Curriculum – A Program for Emerging Self-Advocates with Autism Spectrum and Other Conditions.* Autism Asperger Publishing Company; www.asperger.net. Used with permission.

Internet Scavenger Hunt: The Autism Community
Integrated Self-Advocacy ISA™

My Personal Information:

Your name: _____   Date: _____

Class: _____

Find the following hunt items by conducting text, image, or video clip searches on the World Wide Web. Make a few notes that you can share with your teacher or class. Think about the perspective on autism each item in the hunt represents and make notes on that, too.

Person/Organization	Type of Find		Notes on Perspective
Tony Attwood	☐ Text ☐ Video Clip	☐ Picture ☐ Audio Clip	
Mr. Inevitable	☐ Text ☐ Video Clip	☐ Picture ☐ Audio Clip	
Autism Society of America (ASA)	☐ Text ☐ Video Clip	☐ Picture ☐ Audio Clip	
Global Regional Asperger Syndrome Partnership (GRASP)	☐ Text ☐ Video Clip	☐ Picture ☐ Audio Clip	
Dan Marino	☐ Text ☐ Video Clip	☐ Picture ☐ Audio Clip	
The Autistic Self-Advocacy Network (ASAN)	☐ Text ☐ Video Clip	☐ Picture ☐ Audio Clip	
Temple Grandin	☐ Text ☐ Video Clip	☐ Picture ☐ Audio Clip	
The Autism Research Institute (ARI)	☐ Text ☐ Video Clip	☐ Picture ☐ Audio Clip	

From Paradiz, V. (2009). *The Integrated Self-Advocacy ISA™ Curriculum – A Program for Emerging Self-Advocates with Autism Spectrum and Other Conditions.* Autism Asperger Publishing Company; www.asperger.net. Used with permission.

Making Advocacy Scripts
Integrated Self-Advocacy ISA™

Your name: _____   Date: _____

My Advocacy Goal, Need, or Preference

Briefly describe the advocacy goal, need, or preference for which you'll be writing a script:

Analyze the Context	Write Your Answers
LOCATION: Where will you be using this script? What is the environment like? Public, private? Will you need to request privacy to say your script?	
WHO? Who will you be saying your script to? Is it one person or more than one person?	
DISCLOSURE: Do you feel you need to self-disclose to reach your advocacy goal? If you do, will you make a full or partial disclosure?	
OUTCOME: What outcome do you hope to achieve using this script? What will you do if the outcome is different from what you expected?	
SUPPORT: Will you ask a support person to be present when you use your advocacy script? Will you ask a support person to follow up with you after you have attempted advocating with your script?	
ADDITIONAL CONSIDERATIONS: Add any additional information that isn't covered above yet is important to using your script.	

Illustrate and Write the Script

Use the space provided below to illustrate and/or write your advocacy script. Be sure to write the words you will say when you advocate for your need or preference.

Illustrate (if you need more space, please use a separate sheet)

Write Your Script Here (keep it simple and courteous)

Before You Try out Your Script

Remember that every time you advocate for yourself, you are in an original moment in your life. Although you have prepared this script and have imagined how you would like things to go when you use it, remember that you might not get the results you want, or that the words you are prepared to say might come out differently. In any advocacy moment, it's important to keep an open mind and *expect* that things won't always go the way you want them to. Advocacy is an ongoing process. The success is in attempting it!

Follow-up and *The Self-Advocacy Portfolio*

After you have used your Advocacy Script, assess how things worked out. Make any revisions you would like to the script, then transfer the revised version to your *Self-Advocacy Portfolio* on page 88.

Assessment

A. On a scale from 1 to 4, how effective was your script in achieving your advocacy goal or need? (Circle one).

1	2	3	4
The plan backfired or was a total disaster.	The plan went O.K., but I didn't reach my goal.	The plan went O.K., and I only reached part of my goal.	The plan was a success. I reached my goal.

B. If you chose 1 above, do you feel you need to take another approach? If yes, how?

C. If you chose 2 or 3 above, how can you improve your advocacy script? Make any changes here:

> ***Transfer your successful or revised script to the scripts section of your* Self-Advocacy Portfolio on page 88. *The portfolio is a living document where you can save helpful advocacy tools that have worked for you.***

The Sensory Scan™ Worksheet
Integrated Self-Advocacy ISA™

My Personal Information & Scan Location

Your name: _____ Date: _____

School/grade/program:_____

Which room or environment will you be scanning? _____

The Sensory Scan

1. **Auditory Scan:** Pay attention to **the sound** in this environment. Which of the following apply to you? Fill in as many details as you can in the Notes sections.

   ☐ Background noise is distracting
   Notes:

   ☐ Challenge with number or volume of voice(s)
   Notes:

   ☐ Sudden loud noises
   Notes:

   ☐ Other
   Notes:

2. **Visual Scan:** Pay attention to **what you see or how you see** in this environment. Which of the following apply to you? Fill in as many details as you can in the Notes sections.

   ☐ Light in room is too bright or too dim
   Notes:

   ☐ Angle of light is difficult (from above, below, etc.)
   Notes:

   ☐ Distracted by things hanging on the wall or in my peripheral vision
   Notes:

   ☐ Type of light is distracting or challenging
   Notes:

   ☐ Challenges reading in this environment
   Notes:

   ☐ Other
   Notes:

3. **Olfactory Scan (Smell):** Pay attention to the **smells** in this environment. Which of the following apply to you? Fill in as many details as you can in the Notes sections.

   ☐ Smell from objects is distracting, challenging
   Notes:

   ☐ Smell from person(s) is distracting, challenging
   Notes:

   ☐ The general smell of the room is difficult
   Notes:

   ☐ Other
   Notes:

4. **Tactile Scan (Touch/Feel):** Pay attention to **your reaction to touch or to the things or people you touch/feel** in this environment. Which of the following apply to you? Fill in as many details as you can in the Notes sections.

   ☐ Generally cannot tolerate others' touch
   Notes:

   ☐ Sometimes don't feel pain the way others do
   Notes:

   ☐ Challenges with how things or surfaces feel to the touch (sticky, wet, rough, etc.)
   Notes:

   ☐ Other
   Notes:

5. **Oral Scan:** Pay attention to **tastes or textures on your tongue** in this environment. Which of the following apply to you? Fill in as many details as you can in the Notes sections.

☐ Challenges with the texture or taste of certain foods
Notes:

☐ Challenges with mixed foods
Notes:

☐ Other/Notes:

6. **Vestibular Scan:** Pay attention to **how movement affects or doesn't affect you** in this environment. Which of the following apply to you? Fill in as many details as you can in the Notes sections.

☐ Cannot sit for long periods of time
Notes:

☐ Would like to spin in circles
Notes:

☐ Motion in vehicles is disruptive/makes me feel sick or confused
Notes:

☐ Other
Notes:

7. **Proprioceptive Scan:** Pay attention to your experience of **your body and the space around you**. Which of the following apply to you? Fill in as many details as you can in the notes sections.

☐ Easily bump into others or the walls
Notes:

☐ Need to rock, bounce, or press against other things or people
Notes:

☐ Trouble writing on paper (graphomotor)
Notes:

☐ Difficulty using stairs or walking down an incline
Notes:

☐ Cannot sit for long periods of time
Notes:

☐ Other
Notes:

My Top Three Environmental Needs: Choose up to three results from your Sensory Scan above. You will use these to develop an Advocacy Plan in your *Self-Advocacy Portfolio* on page 91.

1.

2.

3.

From Paradiz, V. (2009). *The Integrated Self-Advocacy ISA™ Curriculum – A Program for Emerging Self-Advocates with Autism Spectrum and Other Conditions.* Autism Asperger Publishing Company; www.asperger.net. Used with permission.

Interview Worksheet
Integrated Self-Advocacy ISA™

Preparing for the Interview

Your name: _____   Date: _____

Name of interviewee: _____

To interview someone in the autism community, you must first decide whether you wish to (check one):

- ☐ Conduct a verbal interview in person or by phone
- ☐ Conduct a written interview by email or online chat
- ☐ Conduct a video interview in person

What type of report will you make?

- ☐ Article (textual)
- ☐ Oral presentation (verbal)
- ☐ PowerPoint® presentation (visual and textual)
- ☐ Video presentation (visual)

Requesting the Interview

When you ask someone to do an interview, you must provide some background information on yourself and your project. This will help your interviewee understand your objectives and will make him/her feel comfortable. Answering the questions below will give you the basic information you need to share when you make the request for an interview. Write your answers in the column to the right.

1. What is your name? Where do you live, work, or go to school?	
2. Why are you conducting this interview?	
3. Will you disclose that you are on the autism spectrum? Do you feel it's important to do so? If so, how will you disclose? What will you say?	
4. How did you find out about the person/ advocate you wish to interview?	
5. What will become of your interview? Will you give a report? Will you submit it for publication?	
6. How would you like to conduct the interview? Be prepared to be flexible. Your interviewee might wish to do the interview in a format that isn't your first choice. As the interviewer, it's important to accommodate any special requests, if you can.	

Once you have assembled your information, call or email the person you wish to interview. Remember to provide the person with your contact information, so that he/she can call or email you back. Once you have permission to conduct the interview, you can schedule it at a mutually agreed-upon time and/or place.

Developing Questions for the Interview

Questions for the Profile

For any kind of report, you must include a profile of the person you are interviewing. The profile can be a brief portion of your report, or it can be the main content, depending upon your objective. List at least five questions that you will ask your interviewee in order to gather information for the profile. This can range from what type of work the person does to where he/she lives.

Your Questions	Interviewee's Responses
1.	
2.	
3.	
4.	
5.	

Questions for the Content

Will your interview focus on a particular topic or debate in the autism community? If so, develop at least three questions you wish to ask your interviewee. (If you have trouble developing content questions, you can always use the self-reflection questions that you answered earlier in this unit.)

Your Questions	Interviewee's Responses
1.	
2.	
3.	

 Now you're ready to conduct the interview! Remember to have fun and good luck! If you like how your report turns out, consider submitting it to the Integrated Self-Advocacy ISA web page for publication (www.valerieparadiz.com/community).

From Paradiz, V. (2009). *The Integrated Self-Advocacy ISA™ Curriculum – A Program for Emerging Self-Advocates with Autism Spectrum and Other Conditions.* Autism Asperger Publishing Company; www.asperger.net. Used with permission.

The Social Scan™ Worksheet
Integrated Self-Advocacy ISA™

My Personal Information and Scan Location

Your name: _____ Date: _____

School/Grade/Program: _____

Which social environment will you be scanning? _____

The Social Scan

1. **People:** Pay attention to **the people** in this situation. Which of the following apply? Fill in as many details as you can in the Notes sections.

   ☐ How many people are in this environment? If it's a large number, give an estimate.
   Number:

   ☐ There are people I know here. Describe how this makes you feel.
   Notes:

   ☐ I do not know any of the people here. Describe how this makes you feel.
   Notes:

   ☐ Other.
   Notes:

My comfort level with people in this setting is (circle one):			
1	2	3	4
unbearable	uncomfortable	not a problem	comfortable

2. **Structure & Space:** Pay attention to **the structure of this situation and how people are distributed in space in relation to you.** Which of the following apply? Fill in as many details as you can in the Notes sections.

   ☐ This is a formal or organized setting. People are seated in rows of chairs or at table(s) or desk(s).
   Notes:

   ☐ I feel comfortable with the amount of space in relation to the number of people.
   Notes:

   ☐ The setting is not formal or organized. People are moving about at will or standing/sitting in groups.
   Notes:

☐ I feel uncomfortable with the amount of space in relation to the number of people.
Notes:

☐ Provide some details on your location in this setting, as well as your proximity to others.
Notes:

☐ Other
Notes:

My comfort level with the structure of this setting is (circle one):			
1	2	3	4
unbearable	uncomfortable	not a problem	comfortable

3. **Content:** Pay attention to **the content of this social environment**. Which of the following apply? Fill in as many details as you can in the Notes sections.

☐ This is a formal lecture or class, one or more people are speaking to the others, who are listening.
The topic(s) being discussed is/are:

☐ This is an informal setting, such as a party or other loosely organized social gathering. People are talking about:

☐ This is a very quiet setting. People are either whispering or not talking at all.
Notes:

My comfort level with the content of this setting is (circle one):			
1	2	3	4
unbearable	uncomfortable	not a problem	comfortable

4. **Expectations:** Think about **what might be expected of you** in this environment. Which of the following apply? Fill in as many details as you can in the Notes sections.

☐ I am expected to participate with others in an organized activity.
Notes:

☐ Participation in this situation is voluntary and not expected of me or others.
Notes:

☐ I am not sure what is expected of me.
Notes:

☐ I am expected to be quiet and listen in this setting.
Notes:

☐ Other
Notes:

My comfort level with the expectations this setting is (circle one):			
1	2	3	4
unbearable	uncomfortable	not a problem	comfortable

From Paradiz, V. (2009). *The Integrated Self-Advocacy ISA™ Curriculum – A Program for Emerging Self-Advocates with Autism Spectrum and Other Conditions*. Autism Asperger Publishing Company; www.asperger.net. Used with permission.

My Social Tendencies

You will use the results of this questionnaire to create an Advocacy Plan in your *Self-Advocacy Portfolio*.

1. Review your Social Scan. Which social aspects of this setting make you uncomfortable (score of 1 or 2)?

2. Which social aspects of this setting are you comfortable with (score of 3 or 4)?

From Paradiz, V. (2009). *The Integrated Self-Advocacy ISA™ Curriculum – A Program for Emerging Self-Advocates with Autism Spectrum and Other Conditions.* Autism Asperger Publishing Company; www.asperger.net. Used with permission.

Focused Interests and Careers
Integrated Self-Advocacy ISA™

My Strength or Focused Interest

Your name: _____   Date: _____

Your interest: _____

	Career #1	Career #2	Career #3
STEP 1: DIRECTIONS List 3 possible career directions that relate to your chosen interest.			
STEP 2: EDUCATION & TRAINING Using the Internet or a library, find out the level of education you need for this job, including special certificates or training.			
STEP 3: SKILLS & CONSIDERATIONS Which additional skills must you have to do well at this job? People skills? Ability to work collaboratively? Ability to work independently? Ability to tolerate stressful environments? Ability to work in challenging sensory environments? Skill in creating social networks with co-workers?			

My Top Career Choice

  STEP 4: TOP CAREER CHOICE

Review the information you gathered above. Using this information, choose the career direction you feel you'd be most capable of, and interested in, pursuing. Keep your sensory and social needs in mind as you make your choice! Transfer this career choice to the Transition Planning section of your *Self-Advocacy Portfolio* on page 96.

From Paradiz, V. (2009). *The Integrated Self-Advocacy ISA™ Curriculum – A Program for Emerging Self-Advocates with Autism Spectrum and Other Conditions.* Autism Asperger Publishing Company; www.asperger.net. Used with permission.

Role Model Worksheet
Integrated Self-Advocacy ISA™

My Personal Information & Role Model

Your name: _____ Today's date: _____

Your role model: _____

Biographical Information
Using the Internet or a library, conduct research on your role model's biography and answer the questions below.

6. Date of birth and death:

7. Country and city born in:

8. Other locations that this person lived or was active in work or other endeavors:

9. What was this person's childhood like? List at least 3 facts.

   •

   •

   •

10. What was this person's adult life like? List at least 3 facts.

   •

   •

   •

Inspiration
List three reasons why you chose this person to research as a role model. Offer information on the person's accomplishments, moral character, or other things he/she has done, written, or said that inspire you. If you find images or quotations on the Web that might be helpful as elements for PowerPoint® presentation, save or record them.

1.

2.

3.

Presentation
Create a PowerPoint® presentation by translating each of your answers above into individual slides. Your presentation should include a title slide, plus eight additional slides to cover your answers. In some of the slides use images or quotations that you saved from the Internet. Present the facts you gathered as bullet points, so that when you do your presentation, you can refer to them.

From Paradiz, V. (2009). *The Integrated Self-Advocacy ISA™ Curriculum – A Program for Emerging Self-Advocates with Autism Spectrum and Other Conditions.* Autism Asperger Publishing Company; www.asperger.net. Used with permission.

Media Analysis Worksheet
Integrated Self-Advocacy ISA™

Your Information & Media Description

Your name: _____   Date: _____

Title of program or story:_____

Type of media: _____   Date of media:_____

Media Analysis

Who is the author, director, and/or producer?	
What is the name of the program, magazine, or newspaper where this media appeared?	
What is the estimated circulation or number of viewers? If you don't know, indicate whether this is prime time television program, a mainstream newspaper, etc.	
Who is the intended audience?	
What is the point of view? (parent, professional, person with autism)	
What is the message of the media, or its intended purpose?	
Is an individual with autism depicted in this media? If so, how?	
What kind of language or images are used to describe autism or individuals with autism?	
Do you feel this media represents autism and/or individuals with autism accurately? Why or why not?	
Do you feel this media represents autism and/or individuals with autism fairly? Why or why not?	
How did this media story or article make you feel?	
Other pertinent information or comments you wish to add.	

From Paradiz, V. (2009). *The Integrated Self-Advocacy ISA™ Curriculum – A Program for Emerging Self-Advocates with Autism Spectrum and Other Conditions.* Autism Asperger Publishing Company; www.asperger.net. Used with permission.

Exploring IEP Options
Integrated Self-Advocacy ISA™

Personal Information

Your name: _____   Today's date: _____

Date of your IEP meeting:_____

Exploring Options Checklist

A. You should feel comfortable and supported when it comes to participating in your IEP meeting. This checklist will help you think about your needs and preferences. Be true to yourself as you consider the scenarios below. Make check marks in all the boxes that apply to you. If you check more than one box, that's O.K. You can decide which of the options is your top choice later.	
Scenario: Make a Check ✔	
1. I can sit comfortably at a conference table with as many as 4-10 people. Most of them are my teachers, my parents, or school administrators. Most of the participants will talk and share opinions. I can sit for the entire time. (This could range from 30 minutes to 2 hours.)	
2. I can sit comfortably at a conference table with as many as 4-10 people. Most of them are my teachers, my parents, or school administrators. Most of the participants will talk and share opinions. Occasionally, I will want to stand up and walk around the room a little, and then return to my chair.	
3. I prefer to stand near the conference table while others are talking and sharing their opinions. Occasionally, I will walk around the room a little.	
4. I prefer to be in the room, with an opportunity to pace. This helps me focus and feel comfortable.	
5. I prefer to stand at the threshold of the doorway while others are talking and sharing their opinions. Occasionally, I will step outside the door for a brief break, then return to the meeting.	
6. I have other or additional needs for attending the meeting than those listed above. I prefer to attend the meeting as follows (add your information here):	
7. I do not wish to attend the meeting, but would like a representative to read a statement on my behalf.	
8. I do not wish to attend the meeting, but would like to prepare an audio recording to be played by a representative on my behalf.	
9. I do not wish to attend the meeting, but would like to prepare a video recording to be screened by a representative on my behalf.	
10. I do not wish to attend the meeting, but would like to participate as follows (fill in your information here):	

B. If you have decided to physically attend your IEP meeting, make check marks in all the boxes that apply to you below. If you check more than one box, that's O.K. You can decide which of the scenarios is your top choice later. (If you aren't attending your meeting in person, skip this section and move on to the box at the bottom of this page.)

Scenario: Make a Check ✔	
1. I would like someone to join me at the meeting for moral support. This person is:	
2. I would like someone to join me at the meeting for support in communication. This person is:	
3. I would like someone to assist me in communicating my personal statement at the meeting. This person is:	
4. I would like to attend my IEP meeting on my own, without a support person.	

5. When I attend my meeting, I will:	a. ☐ Read my personal statement aloud b. ☐ Distribute copies of my personal statement c. ☐ Have my support person assist me in communicating d. ☐ Be present and listen, but not talk e. ☐ Other:
6. When I attend my IEP meeting, I will:	a. ☐ Participate for the entire meeting (This could be 30 minutes to 2 hours, depending upon the number of items that will be discussed.) b. ☐ Stay only for the beginning of the meeting. How many minutes? _____ c. ☐ Have the option to leave any time I choose, so that I can remain comfortable and happy.

 My IEP Meeting Plan

Review your answers to parts A and B above. Summarize the details of your plan for being a part of your IEP meeting below. Transfer this information to the IEP section of your *Self-Advocacy Portfolio*.

A:

B:

Next, answer the questions in the following worksheet, using full sentences. If it's easier to use a computer or other keyboard device, ask your teacher to provide one. When you complete these steps, presto! You'll have a personal statement that you can use for your IEP meeting!

IEP Statement Worksheet
Integrated Self-Advocacy ISA™

Your Information

Your name: _____   Today's date: _____

Date of your IEP meeting: _____

Gathering Information for the IEP Statement

Answer the following questions using *full sentences*. If it's easier to use a computer or other keyboard device, ask your teacher to provide one. When you complete these steps, presto! You'll have a personal statement that you can use for your IEP meeting.	
What is your name?	
What grade are you in?	
How long have you been attending the school you go to?	
What is one of your favorite hobbies or deep interests? Give an example of how you engage in your interest.	
How many students are in your classroom? If you go to various classrooms throughout the day, does the number of students in each class vary? What is the number of students you feel most comfortable with in a classroom in order to be able to participate and to feel comfortable?	
Are there some classrooms you like better than others? Why?	
Are there some classrooms or other rooms in the school building that are challenging due to the environment? If so, can changes be made to the environment to increase your comfort there?	
How do you feel about the cafeteria? Do you go there for lunch? What is it like? Would you want to change this?	
Do you feel you get enough breaks in the day to be able to focus in class? If yes, simply state this. If no, offer a suggestion on what you'd like changed in terms of breaks during the day.	
Do you ride the bus to school each day? Is it a crowded bus, or a smaller bus with only a few students? Do you feel comfortable in the bus? If no, explain what makes you uncomfortable.	

What is it like for you in the hallways in your school? Is it loud, confusing, or do you feel comfortable in the hallways?	
Has another student bullied you or called you bad names, like "retard" or some other derogatory word? How did it make you feel? What do you think the school can do to make it better for you in the hallways?	
Do you have friends at your school? What kinds of things do you like to do with them? Do you ever see them after school or on the weekends? If you don't have friends, would you like the school to work on supporting you in making friendships or joining clubs and other activities?	
Do you like the school you go to? Do you want to continue going to your current school? If yes, why? If no, why?	

Identifying Top Requests

Reread all of your answers to the questions above. Based on this information, try to write at least three simple requests or changes that you would like your teachers and the school administrators to consider. You can begin a request with a choice of phrases, such as those listed here (or you can make up your own):
     a.   "I would feel more comfortable if ..."
     b.   "I would be able to participate more in class if ..."
     c.   "I would be more a part of my school if ..."

1.   I would ...
2.   I would ...
3.   I would ...

Compile Your IEP Meeting Statement

You are nearly finished!

Next, take all your answers from above and string them together into one long essay on a separate piece of paper (or on the computer or other keyboard device). Remember to add your three requests at the end of the text. Your personal statement is born! Be sure to keep a copy of this statement in the IEP section of your *Self-Advocacy Portfolio* on page 94.

From Paradiz, V. (2009). *The Integrated Self-Advocacy ISA™ Curriculum – A Program for Emerging Self-Advocates with Autism Spectrum and Other Conditions.* Autism Asperger Publishing Company; www.asperger.net. Used with permission.

APC

Autism Asperger Publishing Company
P.O. Box 23173
Shawnee Mission, Kansas 66283-0173
877-277-8254
www.asperger.net